Timeless Teachings
from the
Therapy Masters

Timeless Teachings
from the
Therapy Masters

C. Alexander Simpkins Ph.D.
&
Annellen Simpkins Ph.D.

RADIANT DOLPHIN PRESS

Library of Congress Control Number

ISBN 0-967911346

Radiant Dolphin Press
San Diego, California 92109
radiantdolphin@aol.com

Printed in the United States of America

First Edition
06 05 04 03 02 01   1 3 5 7 9 10 8 6 4 2

Cover Art by Carmen Z. Simpkins

*Carmen Z. Simpkins' abstract expressionist paintings suggest mood,
movement, and mysticism. Simpkins has been painting for 75 years.
Her first solo show took place in Camden, Maine, in 1962 at the
Broadlawn Gallery. She has exhibited throughout the world, and her
works are in private collections in Europe and the Americas. Her
work can be seen at her gallery in Clinton, South Carolina.*

We dedicate this book to:
Our parents, Carmen and Nathaniel Simpkins
and Naomi and Herbert Minkin,
Our children Alura Aguilera and C. Alexander Simpkins jr.
and to our wonderful teachers.
Jerome D. Frank
John C. Whitehorn
Carl Rogers
Arthur Combs
Milton H. Erickson
G. Wilson Shaffer

Contents

One of the most valuable training devices in any field is that of making available to the trainee the work of a master.
--G. Wilson Shaffer

INTRODUCTION

Psychotherapy is a noble profession. Those who devote their lives to help others in this way are a vital, positive force for the benefit of humanity. The path to mastery of this art is a fascinating, lifelong quest filled with meaning and value.

The Tibetan Buddhists believe that true wisdom does not disappear; it lies hidden around the world in secret places encoded and ready to be expressed as if in time capsules. In every century this ancient wisdom called *terma* is rediscovered to continue evolving doctrine so that compassionate teachers can help with problems of that era. The work of the masters of psychotherapy in this book can be thought of as *terma*— wisdom that is rediscovered for our time now, to supplement and enrich all modern helpers in their quest to become better therapists. Other terma from other masters awaits discovery.

These great teachers shared their personal meanings to help us grow as psychotherapists when we were students. They were idealists, committed to their lifework, as are many psychotherapists today. Each of these perspectives is unique, as are the individuals who created them. But these perspectives share much in common, timeless teachings We learned a great deal this way and hope that you, our reader, are helped by their words, concepts, and deep committment in your own quest to grow as a therapist. We hope that you, in turn, will help others with your work and further insights.

ABOUT THIS BOOK

The book is divided into five parts, each one devoted to one of the therapy masters. Each part has three chapters to offer the material in several different ways. The first chapter presents our dialogues with these masters. We engaged in meaningful dialogue with each of them. We have tried to bring you into the situation so that you can imagine being there too, hearing their insights firsthand as we did.

The second chapter delves into the important theories and concepts of each master. We spent many years immersed in these ideas and are presenting them to you to stimulate your own thinking about psychotherapy research and practice.

The third chapter offers practical exercises, hands-on techniques, methods, and thought-provoking topics to help you grow in your own work. We encourage you to experiment with the exercises. We hope that you will enjoy the process: Learning psychotherapy is fascinating and exciting.

Part One

Jerome D. Frank M.D. Ph.D.

Photo taken in Dr. Frank's office
at Johns Hopkins Hospital, 1971

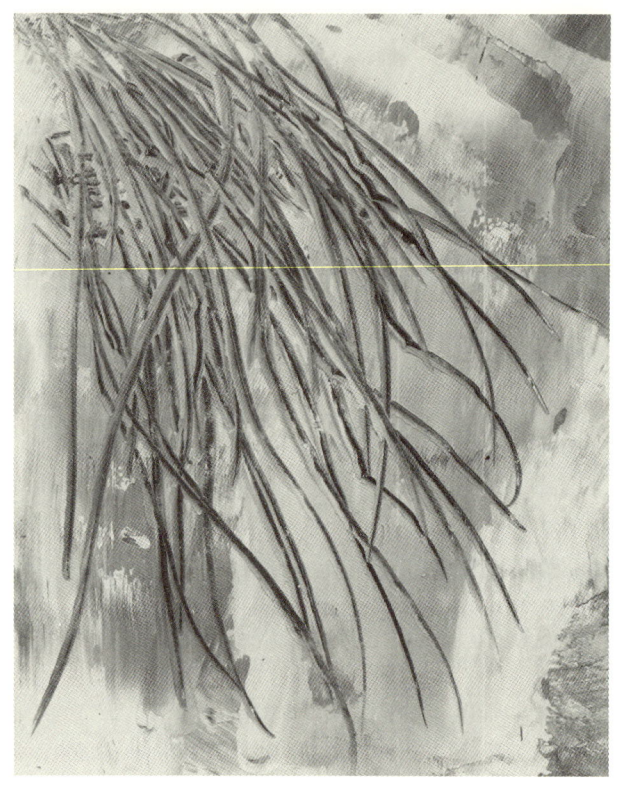

By fostering the faith that heals,
we can enhance our therapeutic power,
a goal towards which we all
continue to strive.

Jerome D. Frank

Chapter One

Searching the Roots

Jerome D. Frank M.D., Ph.D. has one of those discerning minds that can see the broad picture without losing the details. He is fascinated with searching deeper. He has devoted his lifework to looking beyond the horizon, illuminating what others may miss. He encourages us to challenge our own assumptions, to be willing to consider broader perspectives.

Frank was born in New York City in 1909. He received his B.A. from Harvard in 1930. He spent one year studying in Berlin with Kurt Lewin, creator of the field theory model. Then he returned to Harvard for his Ph.D. in psychology. Frank spent another year with Lewin in the United States and then entered Harvard Medical School. He received his M.D. in 1939. He began his lifelong professional relationship with Johns Hopkins University School of Medicine as a medical resident. Except for three years serving with the Armed Forces, Frank spent all of his working years at Hopkins researching, writing, and teaching. He became director of the Psychotherapy Research Unit at Johns Hopkins Hospital. His groundbreaking research changed the direction of psychotherapy forever. Currently Frank is professor emeritus of psychiatry at Hopkins.

Frank not only devoted many years to teaching at the Johns Hopkins Medical school, but also lectured widely. He wrote the influential book *Persuasion and Healing.* His other books on therapy include *Psychotherapy and the Human Predicament, Group Therapy* written with Florence Powdermaker, and *Effective Ingredients of Successful Psychotherapy* coauthored with the Phipps research team. He wrote over two-hundred articles spanning the years from 1931 through the 1990's.

Frank's broad perspective led him to investigate alternative healing long before it was popular. He met with and studied the works of all sorts of healers, including psychics, shamans, and Eastern doctors. Frank's passion to relieve suffering turned him towards understanding the roots of sickness and healing. He felt concerned to help with social problems especially violence and aggression. He pleaded tirelessly for nuclear disarmament and world peace. He wrote a book on the subject, *Sanity and Survival in the Nuclear Age* along with numerous articles. He brought his concerns to public and professional audiences around the world, helping change attitudes, paving the way for new worldwide policies. World peace has benefited from him. He and his many eminent students have helped relieve suffering and improve therapy.

Frank's research unit at Johns Hopkins was one of the first groups to research therapeutic effectiveness. They conducted an extensive study, following and measuring therapeutic progress for twenty-five years. They shook the world of psychotherapy with what they found. In this interview conducted by the authors at Jerome D. Frank's office in Phipps Clinic at the Johns Hopkins University Hospital , he revealed what his research team uncovered, and how the discoveries happened. We met regularly with Dr. Frank for several years until we left Maryland for our doctorate. His positive influence on our thinking was profound. We continue to learn from his broad and idealistic perspective.

On entering his office for the first time, we were received by his cheerful secretary, Franscis Partlow. Her office was filled with file cabinets containing Frank's many papers. We noted a long, beautiful pothos plant with leaves and stem winding around the entire room.

Jerome D. Frank was unassuming but dignified. He was wearing a gray suit, but seemed as comfortable and relaxed in his suit as most people would be in slacks and a polo shirt. He was slim, with wavy gray hair and a broad smile. Frank's office had an entire wall of books and a large desk. He rose from his desk to greet us. He humbly apologized for our having to come all the way to his office to meet with him, even though he was considered one of the top ten psychiatrists in the world at that time. We learned later that he is as famous for his modesty as he is for his insights. He is ethical and always kind.

Frank has tremendous respect for other people and their theories, yet retains the ability to use Occam's razor to trim away the excess and get to the essence. His work helped to bridge the gap between understandings gleaned and distilled from research and the implications for practitioners. Even though retired, he continues to engage in his quest to improve society and make psychotherapy more effective.

We asked Frank how his research team first came to study psychotherapy comparatively, in search of the common factors. He answered, "When we first started our research project, we still assumed that psychotherapy was a modified Freudian approach. We were optimistic about what we assumed to be a foregone conclusion, that the Sullivanian method would be more successful than other approaches. But there weren't that many other approaches in those days. The assumption that most people shared was that making the unconscious conscious would help.

4

Behaviorism was just beginning to come in. The war affected that: you could help people quickly with behavioral techniques. However, that was limited only to specific applications.

"We also assumed that if you varied the forms of different kinds of therapy, you would get different results. We varied it very crudely, individual and group, and in terms of time between sessions. But it was all insight therapy. The results jolted us." His words came out quicker with excitement as he recounted the moment of discovery.   " W e found no significant difference in outcomes. Somehow it caught fire. We didn't know what the common features were, but obviously something was common because patients from all experimental groups got better. That was our contribution," he said. He glanced away and looked thoughtful for a moment.

"Then the whole research program shifted. Most other research was still trying to show the differences between different kinds of therapy. We said, 'Hey look, there are common features going on in all forms of therapy. Let's see if we can define them a little better.' And this gave the direction to the rest of our research. It's like a saying of St. George: 'Research consists in seeing what everyone sees and thinking what nobody thinks.' He smiled, amused by this idea.

"We designed experiments which deliberately invoked these factors as part of the process in order to study them. We hoped that in making these factors explicitly understood, practitioners could maximize them to improve treatment results." They did find that certain factors, nonspecific to any one form of therapy, such as hope and faith, a role induction interview, experiences of mastery, and the therapeutic relationship made a significant difference.

We asked Frank how the nonspecific factors relate to therapy. He replied, "Hope and morale give the patient the feeling that things are going to get better. Experiences of mastery are specific to meanings for the patient. These mastery experiences must be confirmed by real-life accomplishments to be sustained. The self-confidence gained in one area boosts the patient for other areas. The whole thing works together to set in mind a positive drive toward healing and health."

We wondered how this helps heal and resolve conflicts in the mind. "One part of my book (Frank, 1991) that is new is about meanings; that psychotherapy transpires in the realm of meanings. I tried to point to a generic form of psychotherapy that applies to all patients. Then, of course every therapist has his or her own methods.

"Over the years I have become more and more convinced that psychotherapy involves a transformation of meanings. Change meanings the patient attaches to things and the patient will change. It's very similar to the concept of noble rhetoric of Aristotle. There is an integrating force, which arouses emotions and changes meanings. This has a healing effect."

Since we were studying hypnotherapy and suggestion, we asked Frank whether suggestion could be a nonspecific factor. He answered, "I could never formulate suggestion in a way I was comfortable with, but I do believe that there is an element of suggestion present indirectly. If I could, I would include it as a nonspecific factor."

He explained how the assumptive world relates to meaning. "The assumptive world includes one's perspective on the world, feelings, behaviors, and attitudes. As meanings shift from psychotherapy, a change in one's evaluation of experiences and events takes place. Perceptions of things shift, like values and components of the personality. The core person doesn't change but he or she is more hopeful and less anxious." So psychotherapy does not change people into someone else, it just helps them live more masterfully and feel more comfortable and positive.

Frank was a student of Kurt Lewin, whose field theory viewpoint greatly influenced Frank's thought. His three early articles in 1935 on the level of aspiration and its influence brought awareness of the topic to America from Berlin and sparked a flood of studies in American psychology. This became one of the more important demonstrations of field interactions, and has been woven into the fabric of social psychology in various disguises, such as the discrepancy between ideal and real self. (Cartwright, 1959) Frank stated simply, "I think of the person as always interacting with the environment. I guess I am a social psychologist more than an individual psychologist, although I haven't thought of myself in those terms."

We wondered whether a man of such breadth in perspective ever had difficulty in choosing what to research. He responded, "I don't choose a research project, I come down with one!" He felt researching almost as a compulsion to explore and search. The direction of his life has been determined by his commitment to trace the fundamental problems of psychotherapy to their source.

Despite having made certain research choices, Frank has never been a man of narrow vision: "I see myself as walking down the street and looking to the right and left every now and then, at things I can't go into very much, but I know there are things there. Another image I have is of looking over a fence into a field and not wanting to enter the field but knowing there are things in the field that are worth looking at."

Such visions reflect Frank's broad perspective, always open enough to include the possibility that there are new perspectives which will allow another facet of reality to be revealed. He continues to observe and wonder about life.

Frank dedicated his professional efforts to scientific research and yet he retained his objectivity on the scientific method. "I feel that in this field [psychotherapy] it should not be our only tool. It's like a Procrustean bed, which leaves out so much of what transpires in psychotherapy. The effort of science is to study facts, but psychotherapy deals in meanings."

Frank looked to other areas such as rhetoric and hermeneutics to fill the gaps left by the scientific method, careful not to condemn the usefulness of science. Science covers many aspects of psychotherapy well; but important areas lie outside its realm.

As a scientist with a conscience, Frank's personal passion is to rid the world of the nuclear war threat. He presented persuasive and provocative papers to senators and congressmen, to influence policy. His most recent paper in this area was on the bloodthirsty leader. He approached the analysis of their personalities from the perspective of a compulsive power drive gone awry. He hoped that understanding the negative dynamics can free positive leadership qualities, and help to control aggression. Leaders set forces in motion. If they are committed to peace, their nation will follow.

Of these writings he said, "I write as a psychologist, not a political scientist. I have been driven by curiosity in the field of psychotherapy. But with regard to world peace and nuclear disarmament, I feel forced into it by anxiety. It is compulsive. I don't even like these things. There's a sense in which it seems hopeless, and yet that does not prevent me from continuing to try." He felt compelled to be a positive force for peace.

We asked Frank to summarize what psychotherapy research has really left him with and he replied, "Psychotherapy research has been like opening Pandora's box. When everything is released, we are still left with hope. A good hunk is mysterious. Freud was well aware of mystery. I'm prepared to live with mysteries." Frank opens our minds to new questions and answers. Just as Heisenberg's famous uncertainty principle affected physics, Frank's research shows that we cannot take anything for granted in psychotherapy.

Chapter Two

The Pillars of
Therapeutic Effectiveness

All forms of healing
Vast is their scope,
Find common ground
In the mystery of hope.
(C. Alexander Simpkins)

THE NONSPECIFIC FACTORS

Jerome D. Frank and the Phipps Interdisciplinary Research Team set out in the 1950's expecting to prove that Sullivanian therapy was superior to other forms of therapy. The results surprised them. No form of therapy was superior. All worked equally well. People improved, but therapy helped accelerate recovery. Frank and his team hypothesized that there might be other determinants, nonspecific to any one form of treatment that make a difference in the effectiveness of psychotherapy. This led to a twenty-five year research project devoted to uncovering, isolating, and testing the factors affecting the outcome of psychotherapy. The project's ultimate goal was to improve the effectiveness of therapeutic treatment.

Psychotherapy has now been shown to be significantly better than no treatment. This seemingly conservative statement has momentous significance: Therapy works! Though symptoms may remit without treatment, people endure many unproductive years of suffering if treatment is not given. Thoughtful therapists can integrate the findings from psychotherapeutic research with their own understandings, both learned and intuitive, to maximize the effectiveness of treatment.

The study of psychotherapy and its application to patients takes us from the realm of problems to the realm of the problematic, from phenomena to philosophy. Psychotherapists cannot avoid being involved with the nonspecific factors such as expectant hope, faith, trust, the therapeutic relationship, and the therapeutic theory, which profoundly effect therapeutic outcome. Therapy is effective. Why, and how does it work?

HOPE

Hope can be mobilized through symbols. A symbol points to something beyond itself, opening up realms of meaning. The American flag, as symbol of a country, points to the unity of the fifty states, something greater that transcends them. The United States flag is given dignity and honor itself through respectful and ceremonial handling. Burning the flag symbolically expresses protest and anger with the United States. Unless the country changes and a new flag is created, the symbol continues to carry significance for Americans. Symbols channel and direct actions toward goals, utilizing primitive yet influential mental functioning. Reason, language, and logic are expressed in symbols.

When a patient comes to the doctor, the therapeutic setting implicitly presents symbols of healing to inspire hope. A professional clinical office, with diplomas and credentials displayed on the wall, will subtly and indirectly raise expectancies for cure. Rather than thinking of hospitals as places filled with germs of sickness, Whitehorn liked to say that the "germs of health" floated in the air in the halls of Johns Hopkins Phipps Clinic (Whitehorn, personal interview, 1972), referring to the positive experiences awaiting people when they went there.

The therapeutic process itself can become a symbol for healing communication. The atmosphere of therapy evokes the patient's own self-healing mechanisms. The symbolic level can be helpful and indeed cannot be deleted from good therapy. Interestingly, symbols work best indirectly, without deliberate manipulation, as further chapters will show.

Expectant hope has a healing effect. Psychotherapists can and should keep this in mind when working with patients. Freud recognized the importance of this factor for psychotherapy when he said:

> Expectation colored by hope and faith is an effective force
> with which we have to reckon...in all our attempts at
> treatment and cure (Freud, 1953 289).

The mobilization of hope can add power to the procedures and help to make therapy more effective.

PLACEBO EFFECT: SYMBOLIC THERAPY

Psychotherapy researchers have found an interesting paradigm in the placebo effect, which permits us to observe and measure symbolic factors influencing the process of therapy.

The power of the placebo attests to the healing power of hope and faith. Certainly, a completely inert pill should have no effect either therapeutic or otherwise. Yet, there are numerous documented studies showing that many cures have taken place from placebos (Frank & Frank, 1991).

The placebo has been conceptualized as a symbol of healing and of the doctor-patient relationship. One interesting instance of this is illustrated in Park and Covi's experiment. A group of patients were given a placebo and told that it was inert. In addition they were told, "I think this pill will help you as it has helped so many others." Fourteen of the fifteen participants remained in the study and all reported significant improvement. Those who felt certain that the pill was definitely inert or definitely not inert reported more improvement than those who were unsure about the pill. Patients believed that the doctor was trying to help them, and interpreted his use of a placebo through their individual understandings, as positive. (Park & Covi, 1965)

Coué (1923), who popularized self-suggestion, was originally a pharmacist. He found that his customers improved when he told them the medicine was effective and would probably help. This led him to develop an approach that used suggestion or as he referred to it, autosuggestion, to help patients help themselves. Self-suggestion mobilized the same mechanism that he perceived to be at work when he filled prescriptions.

Placebo research supports the hypothesis that nonspecific factors may be more significant than any specific system or method. The study of the placebo effect has done much to clarify some of the more elusive aspects of healing. Psychotherapists can learn from study of the placebo effect how faith, hope, and trust facilitate the therapeutic process. To incorporate these understandings into the psychotherapeutic process, the therapist must go further.

EXPECTANCIES

Psychologists have been interested in researching expectancy as a way to understand the nonspecific factor of hope. Expectations may be considered a form of hope, without desire or wish. Although hope depends on the wish or desire, it does not always include positive expectancy. Often the therapist sees people who hope to get better, but do not expect to. Their experiences seem to confirm to them that they are incapable. They expect to fail. The interaction between hope and expectancy can have a powerful influence on the psychotherapeutic outcome, but the relationship is complex.

Treatment usually raises hopes and positive expectancies. But these variables remain poorly understood, leading to occasionally contrary results. The authors treated a man who had once been diagnosed with stomach cancer and given six months to live. He decided not to spend his last months of life in depressing group therapy at the local hospital. He convinced his girlfriend to quit her job and travel with him on his boat to a pleasure island. Together they cast anchor to savor the short time he had. They delighted in the beauty of the sunsets, relaxed, and enjoyed each moment. As the months passed, he found his pain was reducing. Six months passed, a year passed, and he did not feel worse. After eighteen months his only problem was running out of money. They both were beginning to feel bored, so they returned to the city and went back to work. Two years after the original diagnosis they came in for therapy. Realizing that he had a long life ahead of him, they wanted to work out a better long-term relationship. He felt surprised and delighted that he could continue to enjoy his years. This situation suggests that we consider making diagnoses with a note of optimism. Sometimes, patients will recover and may need to address other issues in their lives. And positive experiences may be healing.

A great many disorders are affected by people's expectations about them. The complex relationship between expectations and outcome has been researched. An experimental study on stress was performed at Harvard (Benson, 1975). It was believed that stress was directly related to heart disease or high blood pressure. A group of subjects were given careful therapeutic education concerning the noxious influences of stress. They were shown how high blood pressure and heart disease could have negative effects on their bodies. They were shown movies and instructed on how to best prevent the onset of these diseases. A control group, not exposed to these seminars, was also followed. Over a ten-year period, the researchers expected that the educated group would benefit, but the results confronted them with a paradox. They found that the group who was given the stress education actually developed more heart disease, stress symptoms, and high blood pressure! The experimental group had a higher death rate than the control group. The researchers hypothesized that negative concerns may have led to negative expectancies, with pernicious effects. Benson's conclusions were that the wise patient should not spend too much time, outside of professional examinations, in self-preoccupation over possible symptoms. Paradoxically, patients may become sensitized to negative expectations.

Patients' expectancies influence their response to psychotherapy. Friedman (1963) conducted an experiment in two places, London and Baltimore. He used self-report to assess how subjects who registered for treatment at the clinic expected to feel in six months. He found a positive correlation between expected relief and reported reduction of symptoms. Symptoms of depression and anxiety were greatly reduced.

Expectations are also transmitted by the therapist, often without awareness. Outcome can be influenced by the therapist's expectancies. In one project, the therapist's expectations for length of treatment influenced the course of treatment. When the therapist expected treatment to last twenty sessions, patients reported improvement after seven. When treatment had no time limit, patients reported the same improvement after fifty-five sessions. (Shlein, 1962)

HISTORICAL PERSPECTIVE ON EXPECTANCY

Expectancy theory has been studied and researched for a long time. Gustav Theodor Fechner (1801-1887) thought of expectancy as set: a muscular tension phenomenon in the body, referring to impulse and thought. He found that expectancy assumes a predisposition in the organism. Russian theory carried this view further, to consider set as a total orientation, on many possible levels. Set is an orientation reflex to the stimulus, in the organism as a whole, as well as in specific areas. (Hilgard & Bower, 1975)

E. L. Thorndike (1874-1949) held that there are innate tendencies and expectancies, as part of the natural predisposition of the organism. Thorndike considered these expectancies to be very pervasive, and spent many years researching them. He believed that learned associations, or "connections" do not necessarily take precedence over innate predispositions, capacities and reflexes, but rather that they compound with them, along with their satisfying or annoying consequences, to influence learning. (Thorndike, 1931)

Edward C. Tolman (1886-1959) believed learning entails the development of representations or cognitive maps. (Hilgard & Bower, 1975) In many groups of experiments he found that when rats could pre-explore a maze, they learned the solution quicker, even though they had not been rewarded for their behaviors. This finding led him to hypothesize that the rats responded to goal directed internal representations or maps rather than simple associations with reinforcement. He thought that these maps involved expectancies that might help or hinder subsequent learning. Latent learning studies tend to support his notion that signs, maps, or representations discovered by pre-exploration can assist in learning. Hilgard stated that there is little doubt that the phenomenon can be demonstrated. (Hilgard & Bower, 1975) Expectancies become learning sets, to help therapy or to hinder it.

Milton H. Erickson utilized what the patient brought to him (Haley, 1967) in his hypnotic therapy approach, often weaving together with suggestions the innate expectancies the patient carried to the situation. He structured the suggestions in a manner calculated to give a corrective emotional experience. Often seemingly mysterious interventions were designed to incorporate these natural innate tendencies, some of them unique to the particular patient, some universal, common to human beings in general. Expectancies can be an ally in therapy especially when positive forces can be set in motion..

FAITH IN HEALING

Faith can help people through difficulties, if not being the cure. Charcot once said, " The centuries have gone by, but the sacred spring still flows." (Owen 1971, 165) Charcot had noted that hope, expectation, and heightened belief all played a part in cures by faith. The Salpetriere was a renowned hospital in Paris, whose prestige probably gave it suggestive influence.

The curative effects of such symbols of healing as a pilgrimage to Lourdes and other examples of faith healing have been documented, studied, and recounted. Janet states, "We have, then, to admit the reality of miraculous cures." (Janet 1925, 46, Vol. I) Although Janet saw limits to faith healing methods, he recognized that the component of faith has been shown throughout history to profoundly influence human beings. These effects have been carefully documented and subjected to critical scrutiny. What takes place in these circumstances invites us to learn from these healing forces.

FAITH IN MEDICINE

Western medicine is based on a committed belief in empiricism that presumes a dichotomy between mind and body. Descartes has often been considered the original philosopher to separate mind from body, but such theories existed even earlier.

The physician is understood as a mechanic of the body that has malfunctioning parts or is battling invasions by noxious agents. Medicines help control or at least reduce the symptoms. Early biological discoveries of modern medicine were so powerful in their scientific promise that they seemed to denigrate the importance of the mind's link to the body. The discovery of penicillin for certain bacterial infections revolutionized medicine and gave added credence to that position. But the early medical model overlooked the importance of the mind and emotions on recovery. Modern medicine includes more.

An opposite point of view has also found a place in the history of medicine: psychophysical parallelism. These theories assume that lifestyle patterns, personality attributes, or sentiments correlate one-for-one with disease. In the history of medicine, psychophysical parallelism has taken many forms. Plague was considered the vengeance of God on sinners. In the 1800's tuberculosis was thought of as an indication of a sinful life and a sign of weakness. Modern equivalents are the cancer-prone personality and the type-A personality. Such correlations are usually more helpful as contributing factors than as primary causes. Parallel does not mean identical.

Based on exhaustive and continuous research, many scientists have come to recognize that culture, mind, and emotions all play a large part in disease. Many experiments have demonstrated the power of the mind in healing. In recent years repeated studies have strongly indicated that it is a mistake to ignore the effects of the mind. (Frank & Frank, 1991) NIMH carried on an extensive project in the 1980's to study the nature of the links between disease and emotions, thereby reintroducing the link between mind and body in Western medicine. (Dohrenwend, 1984)

THE POWER OF FAITH
Religious philosophers have long viewed faith as a fundamental human experience. Faith according to theologian Paul Tillich (1957) is an act of a centered, integrated personality. Since faith requires a quality beyond one's finite being, it requires courage. The content of faith is less important than the act of faith itself. The act transcends the content. It leads beyond individual concern to the truly universal. Faith is a state of ultimate concern with healing power.

Faith brings about integration of the person and evokes a unifying tendency: thus its vital importance for psychotherapy. The therapeutic process mobilizes the faith both of therapists in their method and patient in their own capacity to heal through treatment.

THERAPEUTIC RATIONALE
Psychotherapists learn theory, leading to carefully structured belief systems. In the tightest system, every problem has an appropriate technique. For some problems such as phobias, this may be justified, but for numerous areas of psychotherapy, differing therapeutic methods bring about similar results.

The implications of this research on the nature of psychotherapy might lead the reader to wonder about the function of theories of therapy, and to wonder whether the truth would be better served by discarding theory altogether. Lazarus (1989), a renowned behavior therapist, boldly stated some years ago that techniques should be divorced from theory. Theory was unessential. Later he made available a manual of techniques for situations with patients. He believed that techniques would become a pragmatic approach in themselves, based on what works.

Frank (1970) disagreed. He thought that therapists need theories, not just techniques. Theories serve a number of very real and important functions, even if they are not the obvious functions one might expect.

Theory provides a conceptual framework that gives a plausible rationale with potential for the therapeutic process to take place. Theory offers the therapist a personal resource during the patient's voyage to mental health. Trivial issues such as whose method works better, distract from the fundamental quest to improve therapeutic effectiveness. We all need our theories. No one theory is best. They are all good, depending on how they are used, and with what problems.

Training programs often overemphasize particular conceptual schemes and associated techniques. New therapists benefit by gaining confidence that they have mastered a particular method. But too much attention to theory may lead a new therapist away from developing the truly therapeutic qualities that experienced healers manifest.

The practitioner may find this a daunting task: to have the objectivity to accept that no one theory or belief system is supereminent while continuing to practice as if one theory is. Our faith must rest on another foundation. As Dryud, a participant in one of Frank's original research projects wrote:

> The paradox of the good therapist is, that unless you have some belief in a specific factor, your nonspecific factors don't work. Therefore, the good therapist must split two roles in himself, the therapist-believer following his conscious model, and the researcher-critic, seeing how this process relates to underlying structure. (Dryud in Frank 1974, 81)

So a well thought-out rationale helps the therapist cope with the stresses of clinical practice. Theories guide practitioners in their conduct with patients and serve as the basis for creating techniques, and give a map for the journey of transformation. Theories are important if we keep them in perspective.

THERAPEUTIC RELATIONSHIP

> All psychotherapies involve a particular setting and a conceptual framework that specifies a relationship between healer and patient. (Frank, 1991 xiii)

Frank views the patient-therapist relationship as "both the vehicle of psychotherapy and the major determinant of its outcome." (Frank 1991, 172) Extensive research supports this. One study determined that successful patients in both interview and behavior therapy "rated the personal interaction with the therapist as the single most important factor in their treatment." (Sloane et al., 1975) Some studies have looked at the patient-therapist combination and found that success depends more upon the interaction than the patient or therapist alone. (Orlinsky and Howard, 1980)

Findings from a study on patient-therapist convergence by Schonfield et. al. (1969) indicated that when patients showed improvement, there was a mutual influence of patient on therapist and vice versa. This experience of mutuality is an important component in successful treatment. Research also showed that experienced therapists from different therapeutic schools had more in common than experts and novices from the same school of treatment. (Fiedler, 1953) What they all seem to be offering is an artful relationship through which patients feel understood and able to communicate freely with their therapist. The therapist is experienced as warm, caring, and genuine, essential qualities of a healing attitude. (Truax & Carkhuff, 1967) Privately, therapists share in these common factors. But publicly, they usually take a stand with a particular school.

The personal qualities of therapists that yield successful therapeutic results involve the ability to arouse the patient's faith in them and in their method. Therapists can most easily arouse positive expectancies with their patients when therapist-patient belief systems are somewhat overlapping. Patients begin to feel hopeful that what the therapist has to offer makes sense and will help.

The capacity to heal also has special qualities that elude scientific detection. Some people are better healers than others, for unknown reasons. Frank always leaves room for the unknown in psychotherapy. He believes these somewhat mysterious qualities keep the psychotherapeutic encounter dynamic and creative.

THE EVOLUTION OF THE WESTERN HEALING BELIEF SYSTEM

Although modern medicine is derived from scientific principles, the roots of medicine are found in the mystical healing traditions of ancient peoples. Hippocrites is often considered the father of modern medicine. However, Hippocrites and his father before him were priests of the mystical Asclepiadean tradition. The Asclepiadeans had a profound influence on Hippocrites' formulations.

According to Greek mythology, Asclepius was the son of Apollo and the nymph Coronis. He became so skilled in medicine that it was believed he could restore the dead to life. Asclepius was a kindly and gentle being.

He carried a staff with a snake coiled around it which lives on today as the symbol for medicine.

The Asclepiadeans built hundreds of healing temples in different parts of the world, where people would come to be accepted as patients. The seekers who were allowed to stay were given instructions in hygiene, lifestyle, and nutrition. Most importantly, while the patients slept, the priests would talk to them. Patients gained insights and had healing experiences. Some historians believe patients were hypnotized, others hold that narcotic drugs were administered. It is very likely that suggestion was part of the treatment. (Alexander and Selesnick, 1966)

Hippocrates combined the learnings from the mystical Asclepiadeans along with the rational understandings of Plato and the Sophists to develop his science of medicine. He believed that nature heals the patient; the doctor helps nature along. The modern principle of homeostasis, that the body tries to return to its natural balance, derived from Hippocrates and his followers. The patient's lifestyle such as proper diet, exercise, and hygiene was considered important in bringing about health.

Hippocrates recognized the importance of the mind as well. He conceived of the brain as the seat of the mind. He said, "I assert that the brain is the interpreter of consciousness." He was the first to classify mental illness into syndromes such as paranoia, still used today.

The Stoics and Epicureans developed philosophies that sought to relieve stress: the Epicureans by having as much pleasure as possible, the Stoics by a lawful and moral life, in harmony with society and its natural laws. Both philosophies evolved an ethical principle called Ataraxia, a state of balance and tranquility. It was believed that if people could remain calm and undisturbed by external or internal events, they could be happy. Psychopharmacology and psychotherapy of today are used for the same results. But it is interesting to recognize that in the days of the Greeks and Romans, mental health was induced by philosophy.

In contemporary Western concepts of healing, the physician is thought of as an expert scientist and technician. Psychiatrists and psychotherapists do their best to deliver the expected treatments. Many people have been helped by advances in the genetic, chemical, and biological basis of health and disease. But Frank points out that if the interplay of meanings of the individual with family, culture, and bodily states is not taken into account, psychotherapeutic interventions will always remain insufficient. Medicine will fail if the noxious influence of these other factors sneaks in the back door. They have profound effects and must be accounted for in treatment procedures. Practitioners cannot ignore mental factors if they are to be helpful in therapy.

PART ONE

RELIGIO-MAGICAL TRADITION

> Examination of religious healing across cultures illuminates certain aspects of human functioning that are relevant to psychotherapy. (Frank & Frank 1991, 87)

Religio-magical forms of healing share the same nonspecific factors of effectiveness with psychotherapy. For many cultures outside industrialized societies, including our own native Americans, health is a function of oneness with nature, right living, and proper actions. Illness comes from a misfortune disturbing the individual's relations with spirits. Disharmony, not germs, is at the root of illness affecting the entire person.

Medicine looks for biological causes and assumes that these causes are primary and sufficient. This Western medical model might not be as effective when applied in other cultures. Members of the American Indian community often find themselves feeling alienated and pessimistic when sitting in the waiting room of a Western medical clinic. They usually feel more at ease in the Native American Healer's sweathouse. A Western medicine approach, which seeks to eradicate a headache with an aspirin, might not be as effective to American Indians unless these patients feel they have improved their relations with the spirits. For doctors' healing prescriptions to be effective, they should take into account this lack of overlapping expectancies.

Religio-magical healers believe in a universe of interacting systems. These beliefs permit different possibilities than the Western perspective where each person is separate. Culture contributes to the meaning, interpretation of causes, and rituals of healing for disease. This understanding can be applied to many different cultures and leads to new perspectives.

HOLISTIC HEALING

One Western point of view combining the religio-magical world perspective with the scientific perspective is holistic medicine. Holistic medicine assumes that the harmonious interactive unity of the organism in the environment is healthy. Lack of unity leads to illness. An irritation in any part of the system shakes the whole. Illness is a disturbance in the harmonious balance. Healing involves the restoration of a healthy equilibrium. Interactions are complex and interdependent. Care for a physical condition must include care for the mental and emotional along with the physiological.

The holistic perspective implies the possibility that physical diseases can be affected by mental states. One creative application of this holistic orientation in healing has been researched by theorist-practitioner Lawrence LeShan (1974) who worked out a method of healing through the laying-on of hands. This method takes advantage of the altered state of awareness that LeShan believed common in many varieties of mysticism. The set of assumptions of the clairvoyant state permits the healers to merge identities with patients, transcending normal boundaries and limitations, to facilitate healing of disease states.

The capacity to heal tissue by encouraging healthy growth and development has been experimentally measured. In a set of careful experiments, seedlings were watered with slightly saline solutions held by a meditating healer. The healer obtained significantly better growth than the controls. Frank speculated that the capacity to bring about growth might be part of the natural endowment of gifted healers and therapists. Although this capacity is not usually measured, it nevertheless has been shown to make a measurable difference. (Frank & Frank, 1991) The cause of the effect may escape observation with our measuring instruments.

EASTERN MEDICINE

Chinese doctors have always taken a preventive approach. Doctors were given the task of keeping people healthy and were judged by their ability to prevent illness.

In ancient China, a first class physician was one who could not only cure disease, but could also prevent it. Preventing illness was primary for the Eastern healer. Only a second class physician waited until his patients became sick to treat their overt symptoms. For this reason doctors were paid when patients were healthy and the payment was stopped when patients became ill. To administer medicines for diseases that have already developed is comparable to digging a well after becoming thirsty or making weapons after a battle has begun.

Chinese medicine is based on the concept of "chi", an invisible internal energy circulating through the body via meridians or channels. Proper stimulation of key points along the meridian system can unblock or reroute chi to promote healing. Acupuncture and herbs are used, usually in combination, to accomplish this. (See our book *Simple Taoism* for more detail on Chinese healing)

A broad comparative study *(Barefoot Doctor's Manual*, 1977) found that Western medicine when combined with traditional Chinese medicine met the needs of the Chinese people most effectively. Following this research, a system was worked out to deliver health care by trained,

"Barefoot Doctors." These paramedical healers roamed the countryside to help. They used their skills with herbs found in local areas combined with Western medicine. This form of treatment has helped China cope with her billion population health care problems. These valuable and effective systems of healing have begun to be integrated into Western medicine. Psychotherapy returns to its wellsprings as it broadens to include these perspectives.

INFLUENCE OF THE PATIENT'S BELIEF SYSTEM

Therapists should not disregard the worldview of the patient. Western doctors who do not take into account the cultural diversity of their clients may find difficulty in reaching them. An interesting situation at one teaching hospital illustrates this point. A man born in Sicily suffered from intense nervousness and restlessness. He admitted that he had flirted with someone else's girl, and sheepishly confessed that he believed his symptoms were brought about by the "evil eye". Despite the doctor's attempts to ease the man's disturbance, his cultural belief was stronger than all the reassurances offered to him through therapy. Western medicine was ineffective.

A second example illustrates how personal superstitions may even influence the seemingly sophisticated twentieth century person. A college-educated man in his early thirties was undergoing hypnotherapy with the authors. While attending a party, he was casually introduced to a fortuneteller who predicted terrible turmoil in his relationship with his steady girlfriend. She forecast the end of their relationship on a specific date the following summer. This precipitated anxiety and depression in our client that dominated his therapeutic sessions. He believed strongly in fate and so expected the loss. When the day came, in spite of all the reassurances he was given in therapy, he experienced dread and anxiety until the moment of the prediction. After nothing catastrophic transpired, he felt greatly relieved and was able to put his attention back on his psychotherapeutic work.

Psychological problems can disturb all levels of the person's functioning: social, physical, mental, and spiritual. All healers have a certain role in society, whether they are Western healers, such as psychiatrist, psychologists, counselors, social workers, and nurses or religio-magical healers, such as shamans and witch doctors. The healer evokes healing forces. Whether the patient is a stockbroker or a native aborigine, the same healing forces combined with a different set of beliefs are mobilized. The belief system of the healer and patient interrelate to affect many levels that become strong influences on the patient's well being.

TIMELESS TEACHINGS

THE ROLE OF PSYCHOTHERAPY: COMBATING DEMORALIZATION

All forms of therapy share common features that counteract the state of mind of therapy patients, regardless of their symptoms: demoralization. Frank accounts for this wide range of effects in therapy with a general theory he calls the demoralization hypothesis. Webster's Dictionary defines demoralize as: "to deprive a person of spirit and courage, to dishearten, bewilder, to throw a person into disorder or confusion" Frank believes that no matter what their diagnostic labels, all candidates for psychotherapy suffer from demoralization. (Frank, 1974, 1991)

Frank draws from a number of stress models for his unifying concept. Research has shown that some people who have serious psychopathology function normally, and yet their mental symptoms do not significantly differ from those who do not function well. According to Frank, the key factor that distinguishes those who become incapacitated from those who do not is demoralization.

All types of effective psychotherapy combat demoralization. Though the influence of treatment on symptoms may vary with specific approaches, the relief produced is largely from raising the patient's morale. Whatever the form of therapy, patients gain a greater sense of inner control, independence, and self-determination. Morale goes up as the ego strengthens. And the ability to cope with internal or external stress is enhanced or diminished by the level of morale.

The characteristic features of demoralization are feelings of impotence, isolation, and despair. Patients' self esteem may be damaged as they lose self-confidence. They become distressed as they fail to solve problems of living. They feel rejected by others when they fail to meet other's expectations. This may result in feelings of alienation and subsequent loss of the sense of meaning in life, with further negative effects on their coping capacities.

In studies comparing several different populations who sought psychotherapy with those who did not, all the former showed a higher incidence of demoralization, suffering from social isolation, helplessness or sense of failure. (Vaillant, 1972, Kellner & Sheffield, 1973) The strongest evidence comes from the surveys of Dohrenwend and Link. (1980) They devised a set of scales to determine clinical impairment and psychiatric symptoms in the general population. When they cross-referenced, they found, much to their surprise, that most of the scales seemed to measure one dimension: demoralization, expressed as feelings of anxiety, sadness, hopelessness, and low self-esteem. In a related study they found that scores of approximately four-fifths of clinically impaired outpatients correlated with high levels on demoralization scales. (Dohrenwend & Crandall, 1970)

People do not seek help in response to the symptoms themselves. They seek help when they become demoralized because their efforts to cope with the symptoms have failed. Research shows that people wait several years following the onset of symptoms before seeking therapy. (Farber & Geller, 1977)

The rapidity with which many patients improve in psychotherapy also indirectly supports the demoralization hypothesis. (Frank, 1991) Sloane (1975) found that three-fourths of psychiatric outpatients improved while on a waiting list. Frank offers this explanation:

> Apparently some patients gain relief from any contact with a therapeutic setting. Either they perceive the contact as therapy or they respond to the hope that they will soon be relieved of their symptoms. (Frank & Frank 1991, 39)

Symbols can be powerful when used correctly for therapy.

Patient's emotional arousability, expectations about therapy, and characteristic modes of problem solving are more directly relevant to combat demoralization than psychodynamic categories. Demoralization is overcome when therapists share values and attitudes with their patients while integrating the essential nonspecific ingredients into their treatment methods. Then, they will work together for the best effect.

MASTERY

Psychotherapy offers patients a conceptual scheme that gives order to undefined, mysterious experiences. Torrey (1986) calls this the principle of Rumplestiltskin. Once the correct name is used, the situation is under control. Psychotherapy enhances the sense of mastery and experiences of success, by helping patients to clarify and thereby master their circumstances. According to Frank, mastery is part of all forms of therapy. Experiences of mastery can combat demoralization.

Experiments (Frank & Frank, 1991) by the Johns Hopkins Psychotherapy Research Project on the role of mastery in psychotherapy indicated that experiences of mastery contributed to the maintenance of change. When patients attributed the source of improvement to their own efforts in mastering skills, they showed a reduction of anxiety and complaints after therapy.

Piaget's widely accepted developmental theory emphasized the importance for maturity of learning by doing. Active engagement helps people make the learnings their own. Mastery experiences strengthen these effects. The experience of mastery can vary a great deal. Mastery might be vague or specific, a small step or a large accomplishment. Mastery can involve an emotional reaction, a troublesome behavior, a frightening situation or rules for living. Most important is that these mastery experiences take place, and they are satisfying. And the patient can benefit.

Experiences of mastery may be gained by many varied procedures. Most commonly, learning and reeducation methods are used. One well accepted example, desensitization, can be understood as graded success experiences bringing about mastery. In implosive therapy, the patient learns to confront and survive an imaginative experience of the phobic stimuli. The experience of mastery tends to generalize to the real-life situation. Similarly, hypnosis may teach the patient to master unconscious functioning without conscious interference. Then the hypnotherapist can help the patient's conscious mind to reorient in a more positive way, bringing about corrective experiences.

SOME LIMITS TO MASTERY

Self-mastery is a concept that is highly valued in our Western civilization. As Frank stated:

All successful therapies implicitly or explicitly change the patient's image of himself from a person who is overwhelmed by his symptoms and problems to one who can master them. (Frank, et al., 1978)

Pande, an Indian researcher formerly at Johns Hopkins, pointed out (personal interview) that Westerners tend to be ethnocentric and assume self determination, individuality, and self reliance to be mentally healthy worldwide, but this view is culturally conditioned. Hindus, Tibetan Buddhists, and other Eastern religions look to previous existences for the cause of problems in behavior previous existences. Subsequent reincarnations may help resolve difficulties. Experience of oneness with the universe is more important than individual achievement. Fate and destiny also play an important role. The ego or self is considered an illusion, a mistaken construct. The well-adjusted member of such a society might not be helped by the criteria or norms of Western civilization such as self-reliance; and therefore mastery has a different meaning, since to be able to rely on others is as highly valued as our Western reliance on self is valued.

Research has also found some limitations to mastery's applicability. Mastery experiences were found to be most useful for people who tended before therapy to use inner control for orienting. Patients who relied on others for control responded better to medication than to cognitive therapy for depression. They also rated low in their sense of self-mastery. (Frank 1991, 172) These research findings may delimit the usefulness of mastery experiences to those patients who begin with an internal locus of control. But it is possible to change after therapy to a more self-regulating way of orienting. Then mastery may become useful to these patients.

The practitioner should beware of generalizing any one technique or strategy to all patients. Instead consider what types of therapeutic experiences could be introduced to enhance change relevant to your patient. Individualize treatment for optimum results. But always try to treat your patient with methods known to work.

ATTITUDES AS INDICATORS OF THERAPEUTIC CHANGE

Social psychologists consider attitudes to be a critical link between people's psyche and their environment. Attitudes can be defined, observed, and measured, and this makes them useful constructs for psychotherapeutic researchers. The Hopkins Team reasoned that attitudes are relatively stable and consistent under typical conditions. Therefore, an alteration in attitudes would be significant evidence of psychological change. So they used change in attitudes as one of their ways to measure therapeutic progress.

A number of experiments (Kilpatrick, 1961) led to the understanding that perception is more than a stimulus-response phenomenon. Perception is mediated by a meaning-giving level of assumptions and expectations. For example, the Ames room, which is constructed as a parallelogram, appears normal to the eye because people tend to expect a room to be square. Odd illusions become possible, where one person standing at the lower corner appears to be much larger than a second person of equal height who stands at the higher corner of the room. Cues of perspective trick the viewer's perception to create an illusion that the first person is nearly twice as tall as the second.

Brain research confirms Hippocrates. Peoples' perceptions of the world are mediated by meaning and interpretation. Researchers have found that a part of the brain does act as interpreter, constructing theories to explain why behavior occurs. (Gazzaniga, 1985) The tendency to construct theories and patterns of meaningful integration of experiences leads to taken-for-granted assumptions, expressed in a stable set of attitudes.

Frank developed a conceptual framework for psychotherapy based on the concept of attitudes. Attitudes develop from our capacity to perceive and make sense of the world. "All human behavior reflects the need to make sense of the world" (Frank & Frank 1991, 24). Human beings create a meaningful environment through the experiences they have. Research on perception indicates that people assign different characteristics to their environment depending on what attributes they have learned to associate with them. (Cantril 1950, 73)

HOW ATTITUDES EVOLVE FROM ASSUMPTIONS

Each individual accumulates a set of beliefs and assumptions over time that help make sense of everyday life. This complex of assumptions becomes an assumptive world, through which the real world is experienced. Some of the assumptions arise out of individual experience in the family; others come from school, work, and the culture. Assumptions about people, groups, institutions, and ideologies develop into a system, taken for granted. People become aware of their assumptive world only when forced to account for paradoxes or mistakes. In these situations, the assumptions do not prove as reliable as they had been in the past, and undergo alterations. (Cantril 1950, 87)

DEFINITION OF ATTITUDES

Enduring assumptions become organized into attitudes or beliefs with stable meanings. Attitudes can have emotional, behavioral, and cognitive components, in various combinations. For example, an assumption that we are all part of nature might tend to lead people to protect their environment. They might feel deeply disturbed by pollution and deforestation (emotional component). This could lead them to actively involve themselves in organizations committed to the preservation of wildlife (behavioral component) and to spend time contemplating related issues (cognitive component). Attitudes can be so significant that they may affect the fundamental direction people take for their lives.

CONSCIOUS AND UNCONSCIOUS ATTITUDES

Attitudes are connected with an individual's sense of personal adequacy or inadequacy. Those that give security and promise can engender hope and faith. Conversely, attitudes connected to a sense of personal inadequacy and confusion can lead to demoralization and despair. (Frank & Frank 1991, 25)

Attitudes also concern less vital everyday events and experiences, such as taste in clothes and food, views on one's favorite home team and sports preferences, or opinions of movies and books. Many of these types of attitudes tend to be conscious. If asked about any of these issues, most people can state their attitude on a given subject.

Other attitudes are unconscious, often forming during childhood from implicit understandings and assessments made throughout life. Cultural attitudes are passed along without conscious awareness. Personal attitudes toward the self might be positive or negative. From difficulties in childhood, people may develop low self-esteem; and a belief that they are incapable of handling life independently. Psychotherapy can help change this.

Cultural attitudes are usually held unconsciously until contrasted with another culture. Many people became aware of our Western cultural assumptions when exposed to the Arabic world of meanings during news coverage of the "Desert Storm" war with Iraq in the early 1990's. Arabic allies such as the Saudi Arabians were sometimes disapproving and uncomfortable in social situations with the Americans and the British, who made up a substantial percentage of the soldiers. The differences were temporarily respected and negotiated in order to deal effectively with the crisis at hand. Attitudes concerning acceptable behaviors, the scope of authority, morality, and religion were but a few of the very stark differences between cultures that were attempting to fight side by side against a common enemy.

Consistency with Reality

In order for people to function in a healthy manner, their beliefs and attitudes must be consistent with the surrounding environment, including important others. If assumptions about the world do not reflect the accepted worldview, the individual might be labeled as eccentric or even crazy. Whether this label connotes a negative or positive opinion depends upon the nature of the difference between the individual's assumptive world and that of society. Some of the world's most creative geniuses have been nonconforming to cultural norms. Troublesome differences result when people break accepted laws to commit crimes, becoming social problems. Criminals may not recognize any problem in themselves, because their behavior is consistent with their personally held assumptions. One of our clients was shocked by the attitude of her ex-boyfriend. When they were walking down the street past an unattended open convertible they saw a leather jacket lying on the seat. He said, "Oh good, someone left that jacket there for me to take!" She admonished him for not recognizing that if he took the jacket he would be stealing. Even after a long discussion, he continued to insist on the correctness of his assumption. She recognized that they had profound differences and decided to break off the relationship. Often other people, such as police or families of victims, initiate curtailment of the criminal's actions.

Attitudes can also conflict within the individual psyche. This will often bring people to therapy because they feel troubled by the inconsistency. People with confused and unresolved feelings about anger may be unaware of their irrational reactions. They may think that they believe in being peaceful but find that sometimes, seemingly outside of their own control, they lash out in anger. This inconsistency brings about uncertainties and conflicts. Often people will make adjustments in their attitude to resolve the conflict. Failure to do so has secondary effects, which can lead to demoralization and the social breakdown syndrome. Frank states:

> The aim of psychotherapy is to help people feel and function better by encouraging appropriate modifications in their assumptive worlds, thereby transforming the meanings of experiences to more favorable ones. (Frank & Frank 1991, 30)

TRANSFORMATION OF MEANINGS

According to Frank, psychotherapy transpires in the realm of meanings. Therapist and patient communicate with one another, proceeding for the most part through the words exchanged between the two. During the therapeutic hour, the therapist hopes to induce a change of behaviors, feelings, and thoughts in the patient through the meaningful use of language.

According to the demoralization hypothesis, patients seek therapy when they become demoralized. People who seek help feel that their symptoms are so overwhelming that they despair of being able to cope alone. The therapist must help patients reinterpret their problems so that their difficulties do not appear hopeless. Attitudes about a situation greatly influence the perspective a person takes. Patients who take a despairing attitude about solving their problems will sink further and further into confusion. The capacity to function adequately diminishes until the person is thoroughly demoralized and unable to cope with life.

> All psychotherapeutic schools seek to help patients transform the meanings of their symptoms and problems so as to replace despair with hope, feelings of incompetence with self-efficacy and isolation with rewarding personal relationships. (Frank, 1986)

The therapist offers patients new interpretations of their problems by presenting a rationale for how the difficulties came about and what patients need to do to change. The therapist attempts to help the patient replace demoralizing meanings with morale-enhancing ones.

The therapist's theory helps to guide in how to best manage the patient and conduct treatment. For example, if the patient suffers from depression, the psychoanalyst might look for repressed anger, since analytical theory holds that depression masks anger. A behaviorist might help a patient to reorganize some of the depressing situational determinants that influence and reinforce responses. A cognitive therapist helps the patient analyze and reinterpret their thoughts and beliefs to bring about change in the patterns of cognition that are leading to depression. A shaman might help a depressed patient chase away the evil forces that inhabit the spirit. In all of these examples from both Western and other cultural perspectives, the therapist leads the patient through a therapeutic procedure based upon beliefs shared by both healer and patient. (Torrey, 1986)

Transformation of meanings takes place as a result of these procedures. For example, depressed patients finish treatment with a different set of meanings for their experiences. When treatment has been successful, they feel a renewed hope about the future. In some cases, the best that can be achieved is to simply feel more comfortable within an unalterable set of circumstances. Other times, the alteration of the symptom brings about a broader change through which the patient feels, thinks, and then acts differently. In all cases, their situation has taken on a new set of meanings. This leads to a change in attitudes that raises morale, inspires hope and brings about better functioning. Psychotherapy can take place through many forms. But the forms that include more of these qualities are most effective.

CONCLUSION

All forms of healing contain certain basic ingredients. When both the healer and the patient have faith in the process, therapy inspires patients' hopes and rekindles their faith in themselves and their capacities. Frank's broad perspective shows us how psychotherapy is just one modality of healing within the broader context of effective healing throughout the world.

Frank's devotion to understanding what makes psychotherapy effective can enhance the work of therapists everywhere. We can now believe in the well researched and demonstrated power of psychotherapy and its potentials. Then we may use the influence that psychotherapy can conjure up for cure.

Timeless Teachings

Chapter Three

Applying Research to Practice

Frank's research has shown the importance of nonspecific factors on psychotherapeutic effectiveness. But practitioners often find it difficult to apply these factors directly to their own practice. This section will help you to make the links.

THERAPEUTIC SETTING

Nonspecific factors of hope are communicated indirectly. Practitioners can take some steps to foster hope and faith so that clients will have a more positive expectancy that the treatment will help. The therapeutic setting can enhance clients' expectancies. Think about your setting. Do you have any symbols of healing? Western tradition uses diplomas on the wall or perhaps a picture of a famous therapist such as Freud. Buddhist approaches might have a picture of Buddha. More general symbols of hope and healing can also be used.

Consider the atmosphere. Is it comfortable and inviting? How is the client brought into the office? If you have a secretary, does this person treat your patients appropriately for your treatment? Think about your therapeutic setting and make adjustments as needed.

THERAPEUTIC METHOD

Psychotherapists choose an approach to psychotherapy for many reasons, but sometimes not the right ones. Often we are influenced by our graduate program, our supervisors, or even the latest "popular" method. We must make some of our implicit assumptions explicit in order to make the best choices. Does your method offer a reasonable rationale about therapy that you feel and know to be well supported?

The first step in self-observation is to develop the tools. Most psychotherapists are trained observers. To notice material that is not quite conscious requires an extension of the powers of observation already possessed. The following exercise is drawn from Zen Buddhism. You can learn to observe your own stream of consciousness without interference.

ZEN MEDITATION

Sit with your eyes closed and muscles relaxed in a quiet place. Turn your attention to your flow of thoughts, feelings, and sensations. Notice each moment-by-moment experience. Do not try to control or interfere. Simply observe. If you find yourself being carried away by a particular stream of thought, gently bring your awareness back to the flow. This meditation can be difficult to sustain at first, but will become easier with practice.

MEDITATION ON YOUR ASSUMPTIONS

Consider your assumptions about psychotherapy and then observe your thoughts in this manner. Gradually, some of your presuppositions and assumptions may emerge.

The most obvious influence on consciousness is one's ideas, constructs, and system of thought— that is, your assumptive world about therapy. The therapist can ask, why these theories? These assumptions? What lies behind this as a choice? The answer to these questions involves you and your individuality. Perhaps personal history has influenced you. For example Victor Frankl's experiences in a concentration camp during World War II led him to his system of therapy. Usually the links are subtler and more complex, but are discernable with careful probing.

Ask yourself, what environmental, social, political, and economic influences of the times have also contributed to your point of view. All of this probing is fairly accessible to memory and can be brought out with sincere, careful thought and possibly someone else to listen. What becomes more difficult are the less conscious experiences which have become adopted automatically, without thinking. Both the unconscious influences along with the conscious ones are the foundation of your psychotherapeutic theory and approach. Your personal theory matters. Don't take it for granted.

THERAPEUTIC EXPECTANCIES

Frank encouraged therapists to raise the expectancies of their clients with the opening interview. He called this first encounter between therapist and patient the role induction interview. You can find instructions for interviewing technique drawn from a master of the interview, John C. Whitehorn in Part II, Chapter 6. Positive expectancy should be based on the truly positive when possible, not on false beliefs.

The interview not only offers an opportunity for you to get information about your clients, but also gives you a chance to let them know that you can help.

Confidently communicating that you have proven methods to deal with their particular problem can raise expectancies, thereby paving the way to an effective cure. So first, make certain to yourself that you are using methods known to be effective. Always keep improving and learning.

Think about your own hidden expectancies for helping your client. Do you feel confident with this type of problem? How long do you expect the work to take? Be honest. Keep in mind that your assumptions can have a measurable effect on what will transpire. Does your approach help your client feel genuinely hopeful? Do you feel hopeful?

QUESTIONS ABOUT HUMAN NATURE

All psychotherapeutic theories make assumptions about human nature. You can ask yourself certain questions to clarify your own psychotherapeutic theory. Once these questions have been asked, the rationale for the use of treatment strategies becomes clearer.

One of the most basic questions to ask is what is the nature of humanity? Some theories believe that people are biological beings. Combs, Rogers, and Maslow held this view and their self-actualization theory followed directly. They believed people are like an acorn, destined to become an oak tree. To be healthy is to simply let nature take its course, to fully become what you can potentially be. This delimits the role of the therapist to facilitator, guiding the client to fulfill his or her psychobiological destiny.

Other theorists hold that people are social beings. Frank's theory of the assumptive world assumes that our major learning comes from the environment. Social interaction is the path to psychological health.

Shaffer, Whitehorn, and Meyer believed that people are an integration of the biological, social, and genetic. We live in an environment, but we are individuals within this environment. All these influences are interrelated and must be taken into account. Treatment from this perspective, at its best, involves collaborative work between medical, psychological, and social practitioners to deal adequately with all the different levels.

Another question to ask is whether you believe people have free will or are determined. William James dealt with this topic extensively as have many philosophers over the ages. But it is not merely an esoteric exercise in philosophy. It has very real consequences on how you approach your client. The behavioral view tends to look at human beings as determined by the environmental pushes and pulls. Thus it follows that a treatment approach that manipulates the determiners of behavior will have success in helping people change. But if you take the view that people have free will, your approach must take into account the individual's reactions in order to be effective. Some of the humanistic and existential theories take this perspective. Many theories, led by the psychoanalytic schools, believe that people become determined by neurotic conflicts and that psychotherapy helps to free them. Careful thought about this issue and study of relevant research concerning your method will guide you in your techniques. But most importantly, you should be able to sincerely believe in your method, based on research and experience.

Psychotherapeutic theory in itself is an important factor in effective therapy. Therefore, therapists will do better with a theory they personally feel is closest to truth. Theory should be consistent with deeper assumptions, and these explorations can help you to make certain that you do have cognitive consistency between your deeper assumptions and your working model. When you feel unified with your theory, you will automatically communicate positive expectancy and a convincing therapeutic rationale helping to maximize the effectiveness of your work.

Part Two

John C. Whitehorn M.D.

Courtesy of The Alan Mason Chesney Medical Archives
of The Johns Hopkins Medical Institutions
Photographer: Leonard L. Grief Jr.

*The major task is to mobilize the commonsense
insights that students have already developed
or almost developed, and to help them
in scrutinizing and in organizing
their own insights, and in examining
the relevance of these insights....*

John C. Whitehorn

Chapter Four

A Commonsense Approach to Treatment

As Director of Johns Hopkins Hospital Phipps Clinic, John C. Whitehorn (1894-1973) commanded deep respect from mental health professionals around the world. But when he spoke, he communicated with commonsense; this was in harmony with his approach to psychotherapy.

Born on a frontier homestead in Nebraska, Whitehorn attended a one-room sod schoolhouse on the prairie. He never forgot his humble roots, retaining a natural ease in communicating with people. He worked his way through Doane College in Nebraska and then went on to Harvard Medical School. Following graduation he worked in a biochemical laboratory at McLean Hospital where he focused on the physiology of emotional reactions. These early research projects paved the way for psychiatry's discoveries about chemical and biological components of mental illness.

Whitehorn went on to work at Massachusetts General Hospital, then Harvard Medical School, followed by Washington University and finally Johns Hopkins University. He remained there, as Chief of Staff, teacher, researcher, and therapist. He investigated emotions in numerous experiments with patient-subjects. His successful treatment of psychiatric patients showed that people can recover from mental disturbance if given the opportunity with correct methods. He believed that mental disorders could be successfully treated by psychological means.

Whitehorn wrote numerous papers and lectured widely on technique and dynamics of psychotherapy, stress, and training. His ideas have as much relevance today as when he first began formulating them in the 1920's. His classic paper on interviewing is still frequently referred to as part of psychiatric teaching courses at Johns Hopkins Hospital. Modern demands for technique, diagnosis, and prescription would be balanced and supplemented by a return to the personal, dignified, yet commonsense approach taught by John C. Whitehorn.

We were fortunate to be able to interview and learn from the insights of Dr. John C. Whitehorn at his home in 1972. The timeless spirit of psychotherapy he communicated continues to enhance our understanding.

Footsteps sounded in the hall. The door creaked open.

"Well, hello, you must be the Simpkins. Please come in, sit down, and take off your coats." We entered and handed him our coats, as we looked around and tried to get a sense of Dr. John Whitehorn, teacher of teachers.

A tall, slim, older man inspected us curiously, through his half-rimmed glasses. He was wearing a tan alligator golf shirt and charcoal-gray wool slacks.

We walked into the living room, just left off the hall. It was simple and uncluttered, in traditional decor. The atmosphere was quiet and cool. Plants and the usual arrangement of couch and easy chair faced the front. A small alcove study opened off from the living room.

Dr. Whitehorn followed us into the room, observing carefully. He got a towel for our baby to lie on. We knew our active, exploring daughter was never one to remain in one place on a protective towel, but placed her down upon it hopefully.

He settled in his chair and asked affably, "Well, what can I do for you folks?" He had a comforting way of being kindly while expectant, which subtly invited us to speak. We explained that we had read his papers, enjoyed them very much, and found them insightful.

"Oh those", he said casually. We had brought them with us and placed them on the couch. We hoped to learn more about them and his concepts.

"One paper we particularly liked was on interviewing. You talked of treating the patient as a person and being friendly."

"Yes, I learned that long ago, when I first began as a resident. I found that being friendly and nice was the only way to get patients to do anything." He began to explain himself articulately in simple, commonsense language.

He told us that he had been working on a project, which brought him in to see certain patients regularly. He said, "I treated the patients nicely, like people should be treated. They remembered me, looked forward to my coming to see them, and they got better. Patients don't get treated with much respect by most doctors. They are starved for affection. They appreciate being treated well."

"Why, one time, I was making the rounds, and I met this young lady, dancing on a bed. She danced all day long, did not care a hoot for anyone else, just having a good time. She refused to wear anything but her nighty. No one could do anything to make her listen. She had never seen her parents much. She was the daughter of a minister and was the youngest of ten children. She had been shipped off to fancy Swiss boarding schools and then to college. She had led a very austere life, dressed in black quite a bit."

"I was with another doctor at the time. He said to me despairingly, 'I can't reach her, Dr. Whitehorn.'"

Upon hearing my name spoken, she stopped, and said to me, 'Oh, are you Dr. Whitehorn? I read something by you once. Say, did you ever read' -some book, I don't remember what it was now, but I did at the time. I answered, 'Yes, I know the author well,' and she recommenced dancing. I told her I would talk with her again sometime, then left. She did not say anything more, just ignored me and went on dancing. Well, I did come back and talk to her, and she told me about herself. One day, she was looking out the window and saw a squirrel. She said, 'Sometimes I feel like a squirrel trying to climb a tree.'

I could have made psychoanalytic interpretations of sexual symbolism, but you know, I could really see her point. And I told her so. She smiled and said no one had understood her so well before, told me I was good to talk to, and a good listener. From that day she started to recover and was released from the hospital soon after."

There was an intimacy and disarming naturalness to the man that cast a spell of intensity. It was easy to lose track of time in fascination with the stories and anecdotes he told, illustrating and teaching the art of interviewing. His thoughts and memories ranged back, retracing how he discovered his own style of relating to patients to work his almost magical cures. We could see that when Whitehorn practiced psychiatry, this man was sincerely being himself. His blending of professional courtesy and personal charm was subtle. He appreciated his patients and thought well of them. It was difficult to separate Whitehorn the person from Whitehorn the doctor.

Story after story unfolded. He told of a paranoid patient who had been mistrusting of everyone. "She was suspicious and ornery as paranoids will be. She had good reason for it, no doubt," he said with sincerity. With a disarming compassion he communicated belief in the patient, defending her and being on her side as an ally. It was more than just a therapeutic attitude; it was a personal as well as a professional value.

He mentioned a patient with whom he talked in friendliness at length. As he left, the man said, "You will go far, young man." He never forgot this statement, which indicated to him how important friendliness was.

He recounted the case where he had first discovered this basic principle of psychotherapy. During an attempted therapeutic exchange the patient asked him, "Do you know my Aunt Sophia?"

"No."

"Then there's no use talking to you. You couldn't possibly understand my problem if you don't know Aunt Sophia."

"I later came to know that Aunt Sophia was considered in her family as the dominating, autocratic tyrant. This experience was a major issue with the patient." Understanding Aunt Sophia as the patient experienced her allowed Whitehorn to work with the patient successfully.

Another patient had never spoken to anyone. He was considered a hopeless, back ward case. Whitehorn nevertheless would sit with him, read a newspaper to him to pass the time, and say goodbye as he left. The patient never said a word, not even goodbye in reply. One day, Dr.

Whitehorn was preoccupied and forgot to say goodbye as he was leaving. The man turned to him and said calmly and coherently, "You didn't say goodbye, Dr. Whitehorn." Whitehorn was startled! He realized that somehow, his presence had gotten through. Patients can hear, they listen, and they care, even when they don't seem to. These personal interactions matter to them.

Whitehorn stated, "Nobody likes mental patients usually. Even psychotherapists sometimes want to keep away from them, afraid of them as though they had a cold; To keep their distance they make up labels for patients that don't mean anything, ." Evidently, patients need to be treated sincerely as fellow humans, with dignity and worth, rather than merely dismissed as nonpersons. Whitehorn developed these respectful sentiments further by means of his theory. "A caring relationship matters," he said.

Then, Whitehorn spoke of his professional position as Director of Phipps Clinic at Johns Hopkins University Hospital. "I always wanted to just be treated as a person. People would look away in deference as they passed me in the halls. Why all the fuss about me?" He spoke of himself in a disarming way, as if unaware of the high esteem in which he was held. Instead, he preferred to express himself person to person, relating to others naturally.

He seemed to talk as an equal; as just another fellow wondering at all that happened to him as he simply went about the everyday business of being himself: talented, quietly intelligent, while remaining down-to-earth and sensible. The disciplined professionalism he manifested was unobtrusive and unassuming. His prominent position did not lead him to self-aggrandizement. He preferred to discover his ideas and concepts by observation, experiment, and personal experience. Although originally meant for psychiatry, Whitehorn's methods can be creatively applied to many areas of helping therapeutically.

Whitehorn had a humanizing influence on the field of psychotherapy that was refreshing and candid. He worked diligently and successfully to get psychiatry and psychiatrists the respect of the rest of the medical profession. His wisdom is timeless.

Chapter Five

Discerning the Personal within the Facts

Is there a voice that speaks to us from what is near?
Is there something beyond what seems just now and here?
What we hear, what we see is a function of relationship--
The great mystery
--C. Alexander Simpkins

In simple terms, the goal of psychotherapy is health and normality: to enjoy life and function well, with pride, comfort, and satisfaction. Mental health, according to Whitehorn, involves mutual respect and mature support from others within the culture, not merely pleasing or seeking approval from them. This was a cornerstone of his approach.

Whitehorn conceived of neurotic and psychotic persons as "self-disabled, since the offending organism is the patient himself." (Whitehorn 1953, 5) Often people are not only ignorant of the nature of their self-disablement, but they do not want to know. This is where the therapeutic relationship is crucial to psychotherapy. Psychotherapy is in large measure an aid to people in their own recovery processes when something has impeded their spontaneous functioning.

Whitehorn viewed neurosis and psychosis as inadequate responses to life. Therapy can help people use their best assets to discover more effective ways for living. This can be found by looking to each individual's own best times of functioning, not an external ideal or theory of how people should behave and cope. The psychotherapist who has an interest in and appreciation for the personal assets of the patient will find hidden resources upon which to build recovery.

Therapists should learn about the patient's level of functioning. They can use this understanding to guide the patient to relive memories of better times and bring back constructive attitudes that were the basis for optimal functioning. Helping patients become aware of their personal resources for self-righting was another of the important aspects for cure. This leads to what Whitehorn termed "the corrective emotional experience."

THE PERSONALITY, THE SITUATION, AND THE REACTION

Whitehorn analyzed the neurotic and psychotic process into three elements: the personality, the reaction, and the situation. Neurotic and psychotic reactions are the result of inadequate responses to the challenges of life. The therapist can assess what would be a healthy response for patients by looking at and thinking about their personality, reaction, and situation.

Whitehorn recognized the personal elements of the patient's personality comes first. People's problems always develop through their personality. Personality is the organized system of sentiments taken from culture, blended, and based in the individual with his or her genetic constitution. These sentiments evolve as people and temperaments mature. Psychotherapists should take an interest in personality. Whitehorn systematically instructed in basic principles of personality as well as techniques for working with personality. Each personality contains potential resources.

Whitehorn considered maturity relative to definite stages of personality development. He divided these stages into general categories of infant, child, early adolescent, late adolescent, and adult levels. Normal reactions for one level are inappropriate at another level. Psychotherapists can learn more about their patients by noticing which maturity levels are reflected in the patient's responses during therapy. The psychotherapist assesses patients' level of maturity together with their personal meanings to help guide therapeutic strategy.

Patients construe their situation in a personal way and then have their own reactions to this experience. When understood from the patient's perspective, the reaction might not appear inappropriate, but makes sense. These understandings can be used therapeutically.

Whitehorn questioned standardized, formal categorization of reactions. Usually the reaction was to some intensely intolerable traumatic situation. Patients create neurotic or psychotic reactions that alter their experience of the situation enough so that they can cope. At the time, diagnosis was in terms of categories, such as paranoid schizophrenia, etc. Whitehorn's interpersonal diagnosis tried to grasp the meaning of the patient's relationship to the traumatic situation.

During the early period of psychoanalysis, psychotherapists were searching for causes. Whitehorn believed that this kind of thinking implied psychic determinism, which to him was more an act of faith than of fact. Numerous conflicts interact to arrest the personality. But in searching for causes, the patient's course of therapy and rapport with the therapist can be easily lost. And furthermore, patients are very good at finding causes but achieving nothing. Etiology may be interesting but is usually not useful for therapy.

Instead, Whitehorn believed that in conversation with the patient, the psychotherapist will find a wealth of symptomatic anecdotes that express the pathological attitude, rather than cause it. More important than searching for the cause is the development of an understanding of the motivating meaning in the patient's life situation to which the neurotic reaction is a response. Whitehorn spoke out ahead of his time for a new emphasis in psychiatry: the personal meaning.

The therapeutic session offers a milieu in which mutual understanding between patient and therapist can grow and thrive. The concerned professional psychotherapist attempts to reach into the world of meanings of the patient, to understand the uniquely personal meaningfulness of neurotic or psychotic reactions. Whitehorn believed that mutual understanding was primary, arrived at through exploring the emotional need and meaning of the behavior rather than its cause and effect. This exploration constitutes the beginnings of a corrective emotional experience.

Searching for the meaning of reactions is also important in planning therapeutic strategy. Whitehorn studied his patients to discover their unique issues, themes of conflict, and dissatisfactions. Patients are best helped by nonspecific individualistic strategies that inspire normal hopes, expectations, and attitudes. Therapeutic strategy must be based on what is normal in a patient's personality. It must also take into account the emotional level of maturity or immaturity of the patient and the values and gains of the neurotic symptoms.

Whitehorn evaluated his patient to discover unused potentials for coping and to help to resolve issues more effectively. Strategy aims to enhance the healthier reactions within the unique lifestyle of the patient and promote maturity. After formulating strategic aims, the therapist decides the means of achieving those aims through various techniques.

Whitehorn emphasized that pathology was not the main province of the psychotherapist and never was. The path of therapy must be through what is normal and positive to the patient, not in terms of negative functioning or illness. Therefore, to treat patients in this manner, the therapist must find the normal, or potential for normal, for that individual. This requires an ability to understand each patient's personal issues, group loyalties, affection needs, and personal meanings. Sometimes simply listening and reaching a mutual understanding is enough. Sometimes it takes much study to disentangle the healthy attitudes from those that trigger neurotic reactions. Each patient has his or her own unique potential for health.

If the patient comes to a session more disturbed during the course of therapy, the psychotherapist can use this opportunity to compare the patients' attitudes and meanings in the present disordered situation with meanings during past times of better functioning. Whitehorn was able to follow his patients in the rhythms and fluctuations of health and illness, using this sensitivity at times as a barometer of the healing process. He was known to have an uncanny ability to predict the likely hallucinations of his patients in the immediate future, thus demonstrating that he was truly staying in touch with the patient's meanings during the course of therapy. He would use this predictability as a criterion for grasping meaning. His common sense formulations encouraged deep contact with the patient's personal world of experiencing. He shared his understandings with the patient when appropriate.

THE HEALTHFUL BENEFITS OF STRESS

Whitehorn analyzed the situation side of neurosis in terms of stress. Interest in stress began with the many war neuroses that developed in reaction to the very real situational stresses in World War II. Stress came into use as a concept during the war. Notions of stress through psychological shock replaced combat terminology, "shell shock" i.e. brain damage from the shock of shells exploding nearby.

Whitehorn found that mental health was quite possible under stress. In fact, many people during World War II became healthier when challenged by stress. He quoted Gillespie (1942), stating that the British, exposed to bomb raids, had less need for psychotherapy. Some people were significantly better functioning individuals under these conditions. Perhaps they took the opportunity of the stressful situation as a way to overcome their sense of failure and inferiority, becoming more capable and successful in response.

Wolff (Whitehorn, 1956) studied a man with a hole in his stomach from a war wound that allowed for direct observation of his physiological reactions to stress. Wolff hypothesized that the fear of a situation is the critical factor in understanding stress, not the situation itself. Whitehorn applied this to mental health. Whether the patient suffered from psychosis or neurosis, both are mediated by personal meanings in the situation, regardless of the factor of stress. The expectation of danger is what brings stress, rather than danger in itself. Dread of loss of self-esteem, for example, can often be more damaging than the actual loss. When one is fearful, anxious, worried or fatigued, coping with stress becomes more difficult.

Whitehorn pointed out the value of stress as a challenge to be addressed and mastered. He assisted his patients in searching out their personal resources to make stress a learning and growing experience. He called this positive use of stress, "purposeful personal striving". He wrote that life without struggle and effort without stress and anxiety can be a stale and meaningless existence. (Whitehorn, 1956)

According to Whitehorn, Toynbee's notion of challenge and response as creating history is relevant to understanding the nature of humanity and stress. Avoiding stress can be harmful. Stress that can be tolerated in a healthy manner may even prove to be beneficial. Psychotherapy consists in helping patients to tolerate stress by responding more courageously to the difficulties in life—to "right themselves."

PART TWO

INSIGHT

> Some think that insight means finding out the errors in the patient's operations of mind and informing him about them...It is seemingly logical but experimentally quite an unjustified supposition that real learning can occur simply through the beating of verbally meaningful insights upon the ear drum. (Whitehorn 1947, 634)

Insight to Whitehorn meant simply that the patient gained or regained the capacity to listen and hear. Insight is not a miraculous technique or an object that you have. Insight means a process of opening up that changes the patient's life. Patients can be thought of as having bandaged their wounded ego to protect themselves, shutting out the world. To eventually reach the patient, bandages have to be gradually loosened; so then the wounds can be cleansed. Insight is the by-product, not the instrument of cure.

Whitehorn believed it often was not necessary to work on problems or conflicts openly in consciousness. Therapy does not always require making the unconscious conscious, or developing insight into the conflict by bringing it to consciousness in order to banish it. Encouraging a corrective emotional experience through the therapeutic relationship can bring relief and cure, without conscious insight. Conflicts can also be worked through unconsciously to the point when they can be then consciously tolerated. Whitehorn often tried to blend the two methods, resolving the conflict enough on the unconscious level to make it not so intolerable or difficult to cope with and accept. Then sometimes it might be brought to the surface and dealt with through awareness and insight. At other times this was not deemed necessary. The patient might not need to understand.

THERAPEUTIC RELATIONSHIP

Therapy takes place through the vehicle of the therapeutic relationship. Whitehorn stated:

> People can sometimes endure to take off their concealments and look at themselves in the doctor's presence, in a way they do in few other situations. If the doctor can stand the view, the patient can too. Some doctors can't stand it, —they are made very uncomfortable by raw human nature. Such a doctor should not try to do psychotherapy...Those who have to steel themselves to endure the sordid revelations of human impulses do not do very good psychotherapy. It seems to require a fairly robust faith in the human race, —a faith which may grow with a doctor's experience,

as his knowledge of his patients' lives broadens and deepens. (Whitehorn 1948, 13)

The rapport of mutual understanding is initiated through the therapist's sincere willingness to understand the patient, and maintained through the subsequent bond that develops.

A twenty-five year study with Barbara Betz of therapists with schizophrenic patients found that certain patterns of interaction lead to better results. Although patients may have genetic temperamental factors affecting them, their relationship with the therapist makes a significant difference in how they live their lives. An active, positive role with patients was most effective. They called this pattern "active personal participation." These therapists used initiative in their sympathetic inquiry. They could express honest disagreements, challenging patients' self-deprecatory attitudes, and set realistic limits to what is acceptable behavior. They expected that patients have the potentiality for respectful, independent action. In the best therapeutic relationships, neither the therapist nor the patient has to submit to the other. (Whitehorn & Betz, 1957, 1960)

Active personal participation in the patient's world of meanings is important in releasing spontaneity and healthy emotional reactions in patients. Whitehorn tested his theory in 1935 to determine which was more emotionally arousing: probing issues of personal significance to the patient or probing standardized issues considered to be generally important. He found that talking about matters of personal significance led to greater emotional responsiveness. From this project, Whitehorn developed a style of speaking casually with patients about such subjects as golf, cartoon characters or whatever was meaningful to his patients. He found these conversations very useful in determining patients' values, attitudes, relationships to their environment, and their possible symbolic significance.

Patients reveal much about themselves if the therapist listens sensitively and asks the right questions. Discussions about everyday personal interests, for example does the patient prefer modern or classical art, allow the therapist into the world of the patient. Once there, the patient's clashes between attitudes, loyalties, and needs from others can be observed and personal meaning grasped.

People react to people. Therefore, the therapist's personality has a definite effect upon the reactions of the patient to therapy. These reactions concerning the therapist's contribution should not be ignored. They should be accepted, observed and used for the benefit of patients.

Humility and modesty are qualities psychotherapists need. If they want the best results, they must have respect and faith in the powers and resources the patient can develop. At certain points in therapy, therapists can challenge patients to surpass their limits on feelings and personality. The patient responds to the therapist as a human being and expects consideration and respect in return. If given appropriately, this breaks the usual pattern for patients. Some neurotic and psychotic patients mistrust themselves and impose a depersonalization of themselves in their conduct. Others in their social network rarely respond with heartwarming reactions that bring self-confidence and encouragement. The healthy therapeutic relationship interrupts this cycle for the patient, creating a corrective emotional experience that has a stabilizing effect.

The psychotherapist should remember that patients carry the cure for their own disease. Therapists do not cure their patients. Patients cure themselves, just as they disable themselves with symptoms. Working together in respectful, mutual consideration, patient and therapist can discover more effective ways for patients to right themselves and live life symptom-free. This takes place within the vehicle of influence—the therapist-patient relationship.

USE OF ANXIETY IN PSYCHOTHERAPY

Whitehorn defined anxiety as physiological arousal with inhibition. One part of the pattern is unacceptable impulses and the other part of the pattern is "don't." The therapist needs to recognize these impulses and mobilize the patient's resources to decisively deal with them.

It is better to be indirect because patients seldom understand the sources of their own anxieties, especially when deep-seated. Whitehorn looked for the initial anxiety that precipitated the neurotic reaction. Usually it is forgotten through the patient's self-absorption. If the therapist assesses that the neurosis results from an inadequate way of dealing with life situations, the support of the psychotherapist may be necessary before the patient can face this. Confrontation is usually premature.

The psychotherapist should try to look for answers to the following questions in the patient's statements: "What anxiety is being answered by the patient's pattern of symptoms? By what means has the patient met this anxiety problem in the past?" The psychotherapist can then work out a strategy for the present to help the patient find more mature answers without neurotic and psychotic reactions.

THERAPEUTIC USE OF SELF

The psychotherapist is a model for the patient, an example of stability, poise, serenity, and a better way of life. Through subtle means, the therapist can become a powerful influence in the patient's life. However, therapists must beware of developing a personal "Jehovah Complex", a desire to accomplish miracles, be prophetic, and extend control over the patient, which will usually lead to frustration with the patient's neurotic behaviors. Patience, "sensible humility", and respect for the powers that can develop in people will help the therapist to help the patient more effectively.

The most potent biological remedy for neurosis is the patient's personality. Just as he is the disease-carrying agent, so is he also the cure. The physician can only realize that, and then he can curb his Jehovah complex—his omnipotent tendency to cure by advice and domination.   (Whitehorn 1947, 632)

Whitehorn was committed to becoming a positive influence in psychotherapy for his students and for psychiatry as a respected branch of the medical sciences. Rather than promoting a particular method, he promoted values and attitudes that he felt would lead to more effective approaches. By using a simple set of constructs with a good fit to reality, the rationale of the therapist becomes peripheral, the background of therapy. This will leave room for other important variables of effectiveness to enhance the therapeutic process.

Whitehorn believed that the values of the doctor would have a subtle influence on the course of therapy. For example he thought that if the psychotherapist believed in free will he would be able to help the patient discover his range of choices in his circumstances and face his limitedness with dignity and courage, to evolve in his individual capacity for autonomy. But if the psychotherapist was too concerned with the causes and determiners of patients' problems, patients might not be encouraged to explore their options. If all is predetermined, a choice between possibilities is illusory, if not impossible. Whitehorn considered predetermined attitudes a probable source of obstruction to therapeutic progress.

Whitehorn thought that values had to be deeply felt and sincerely believed, not just insincerely practiced and imitated. Patients sense and react to the values of the therapist even if held in private. Well-intentioned professionals should examine and come to terms with their own personal values.

CONCLUSIONS

Whitehorn's concepts, simple as they may seem, add a deeper dimension to psychotherapeutic work. Professional acumen is not easy to teach, but it can be developed with sensitive attention to the kinds of skills Whitehorn encouraged. Whitehorn's quiet, dignified manner was an effective camouflage for brilliant, empathic analysis. He was easily at home in the personal worlds of his patients. He radiated qualities of understanding and sympathy, as well as registering the personal meaningfulness of each individual patient with whom he worked. He was compassionate, always caring deeply for his patients. He was masterful in simplifying subtle and delicate matters so as to help teach the art of interviewing and therapeutic strategy, without downplaying the fundamentally complex nature of psychotherapy. We can gain in our own work, by attuning our awareness to "the person who is the patient," and let the patient's inner meanings be our guide.

PART TWO

Chapter Six

The Art of Interviewing

One of Whitehorn's most memorable contributions was his sensitive work with the psychotherapeutic interview. The interview can be a "degradation ceremonial" (Frank & Frank, 1991) that runs the risk of humiliating the client to the detriment of the therapeutic progress. If approached carefully from the orientation Whitehorn suggested, the interview can become an opening inroad to success in any kind of therapy.

Whitehorn's way of treating his patients with respect and interest has become the cornerstone of modern psychiatric interviewing. As Kaplan and Sadock state in their contemporary textbook on modern psychiatry, "The psychiatrist must be able to convey concern, empathy, respect, and competence to the patient in order to create a rapport and trust that allow the patient to speak honestly and intimately" (Kaplan & Sadock 1996, 1). We invite you to experiment with Whitehorn's method of interviewing and try the exercises to supplement your own interviewing techniques.

Whitehorn, who theorized from a medical frame of reference, believed that when the psychotherapist interviews a patient, he does the psychological equivalent of a medical history. He verbally percusses and then listens to the qualities of the response. This is similar to how a physician taps tissues, listens to the sounds and observes reflex responses during a physical examination.

Whitehorn departed radically from the mere questionnaire interview. He believed that the questionnaire approach will not elicit much information of significance and can run the risk of alienating the client from further treatment. One of the pitfalls of professionalism can be concern with obtaining the correct information and filling in the blanks on the interviewform at the expense of the client's welfare. Clients are likely to disclose themselves when the therapist listens sincerely to what the client says. The interviewer is a participant-observer and should study the client's personality in action. The interaction gives excellent opportunity to understand and empathize with the client.

49

On the other hand, the therapist is not encouraged to jump right in with advice. The relationship is in process of being developed in the interview, and this is important to develop first. Aloof or contemptuous attitudes can interfere with establishing rapport. Alert and sympathetic consideration is best.

OPENING THE INTERVIEW

Clients come into the interview with a problem that concerns them. Something has bothered them enough to seek therapy. The therapist must be certain to address this concern. Even if the therapist thinks that it might be better for the client to gain self awareness, understand repressed problems, become calmer, change a behavior, or any other therapeutic goal which therapists hold dear, first and foremost the client must be listened to.

Look for ways to communicate interest in the client 's welfare. Express concern for how symptoms, behaviors, and frustrations may not be as weird or mad as the client may think. It can be very reassuring to clients that their difficulties are not unique, and that there are probably circumstances and determinants that have brought them to this point.

The presenting problem, or "chief complaint" is the usual way of beginning a therapeutic interview. The soundest basis for a conversation of mutual interest usually rests there, and many clients begin talking about their problem spontaneously. Clients may disclose a great deal by how they talk about their presenting problem. Whitehorn called this "Scrutiny of the patient's personality in action" (Whitehorn, 1944). This means an interaction between therapist and client, in which the therapist is an active participant-observer. The client's own way of understanding the problem is important, as well the expectancies that the client has about the therapist, therapeutic setting, and getting help.

EXERCISE TO UNDERSTAND THE PRESENTING PROBLEM:

Ask clients to recall the first time they had the problem. Have them describe the memory and observe how they express their feelings and thoughts. Ask, for example, "What do you feel as you recall that?" Another way is to approach indirectly. This may vary widely. Ask what it would be like for someone to have such a problem, and then notice whether any other memories or thoughts come to mind. This will usually lead to further observations about the problem and its development.

CLARIFYING EXPECTANCIES

Expectancies are clarified at the beginning and the end of the interview. When clients first come in for therapy, they have certain expectations for help. The therapist may need to clarify in the beginning that he or she is there to help, ask what the client expects the therapist can do about the problem, and what kind of help the client will take. Clients do not often know about the resources available. Give a sense of what they can expect as well as to understand what they do expect. Then the therapist can guide the client in how to best use the available help.

After you have listened carefully to the client's description of the problem, summarize how you construe the difficulty. Make certain that you show what you believe to be the major difficulty in living. Present this gently, so as to reduce the anxiety and defensive needs of the client. Try to imply that the interview makes sense and that you understand. If you feel confident you can help, make it clear that you have the resources and methodology available to help.

Deeper core problems may be revealed later on in therapy. By forming a bond based upon the client's presenting problem you forge the possibility for a lasting therapeutic rapport that will permit eventual confrontation of more central issues. The bond will also give you a starting point to collaborate together.

WHAT TO COVER

The standard interview includes certain well-accepted categories that should be covered. These include identifying data (client's name, age, occupation, etc.) family history, history of the present problem, and a personal history. In addition to these important sources of information, Whitehorn guided practitioners to also listen to the subtler qualities coming from the client.

The target complaint is usually an effective way to begin an interview. Once you have adequately heard the complaint and communicated to the client that you understand, begin to ask other questions to fill out your understanding. Whitehorn believed that there are six basic categories of information that should be covered and observed to expand on the standard data you receive in the interview. He called this second assessment the Personal Diagnostic Formulation, PDF. (Whitehorn, 1944)

1) General attitude, appearance, and behavior. Take note of clients' attitudes to their problems. What brought them to treatment? What was going on in their life before coming to therapy?

2) Stream of speech. Not what the client says, but the manner of formulating and communicating thoughts.

3) Emotional reactions and mood.

4) Content of thought and personality trends. This does not include everything the client thinks, but particularly those ideas that seem to preoccupy the client. Take special note of those thoughts that are stubbornly held against the general opinion of the client's social group and leaders.

5) Orientation, mental grasp, and capacity

6) Insight and judgment

Whitehorn performed most of his interviews at a psychiatric hospital where these were the most relevant questions. Practitioners in other settings must consider the needs of their situation with clients. A school counselor might need to question a student with learning problems more carefully about intellectual capacities. A client with a drug problem should be carefully questioned about drug use history. Each therapist must determine the kinds of data that will be most helpful for treatment. Remember to look for multilevel of response—behavioral, emotional, and cognitive.

USE OF SELF

You can learn a great deal about the client by taking an inward glance into your own feelings during the interview. Notice any unusual thoughts, feelings or associations that might occur to you, especially if they seem unrelated. Your own reactions can be clues to how the client manipulates the environment.

HOW TO DEAL WITH RESISTANCE

Some clients avoid talking about their problem. With time and practice, the therapist learns to elicit the relevant material in any conversation. Therapists should make it clear to the client that they are very interested in hearing the client's own side of the story. It is important that the therapist express this as a sincere interest, not just a manipulation. Clients will quickly recognize if the therapist only pretends to be interested, which may then backfire. Be willing to deal with your own resistances, too.

A response is necessary to draw the client out. The "blank screen" technique is useless during an interview. Some advice and suggestions are inevitable, and the response of the client gives you more information. Be aware of what your statements imply. You can learn about your clients by how they interpret your advice.

PART TWO

Peripheral topics can become focal points to discuss fundamental personal issues. People express themselves no matter what they are talking about. Listen carefully not just to what is said, but also to what is implied. When you have clients who are reluctant to talk about anything personal, strike up a conversation about something nonthreatening that is of interest to them. As you draw them out, think of their remarks like a projective test. Even with innocuous seeming topics like the weather, sports, or art, clients will express their personality as they become more comfortable in the situation.

Listen to "irrelevant talk" such as, "Oh, you probably think I'm stupid," and look for possible implied self-accusations the client may be evading. As you begin to hear several similar types of reference, you gain further clues. Notice all evidence to find out the nature of the implied accusation or guilt against which the irrelevant talk or behavior could be an evasion or self-justification.

Try to avoid unprofitable arguments. Some clients will try to twist around interest in their reactions, provoking with, "Oh, you think I'm abnormal, do you?" In such cases, you can ask, "What suggested that to you?" And ask about meanings gently, to evoke information. Emphasizing concern for clients' welfare and how their human interests and frustrations affect them can be enough.

EXERCISE IN "TRIANGULATION"

Your client communicates with you on many levels. If the interview is sidetracked by what seem irrelevant remarks, do not always ignore them and insist on following a narrow path to the facts. At times, allow wandering off track but be alert to potential inner logic. Learn to use statements that overlap in meaning or intent like a surveyor to find deeper implied concerns. Take two of the client's similar irrelevant statements, which seem inappropriate or out of context and try imagining them as possible replies to a third. This is like the method known as triangulation that surveyors use with their instrument to find a spot or boundary. Listen carefully and observe if a similar pattern repeats. You may then construct a hypothesis and test it out gently with questions or remarks. It is better to steer the same course the client has gone, to even repeat the words the client has used. Facts will come of themselves, and there is always plenty of opportunity to find them out. Triangulation can be used not just with what the client says, but also from

53

expressive movements. Notice voice tones and gestures. Be willing to imaginatively enter the inner world of the client.

Conflicts will be uncovered, but the psychotherapist will do best to look for the personal meaning of the conflict for the client. Notice how your clients refer to themselves. What statements do they make about themselves? This may help you grasp the personal meaning of their behavior.

CLOSING THE INTERVIEW

When the time is up, or you feel that you have gotten all the information you need, the interview must be closed. It is helpful to summarize briefly so you are certain you understand your client, and communicate your understanding to begin the process. You may present the treatment plan, for example, ten weeks and then a reassessment. If you feel genuinely optimistic about helping, be sure to repeat to your client that you can help, implying also that there is hope.

Notice any little remarks clients make just as they are about to leave. Usually guarded clients feel a sense of relief when the session is ending. Sometimes these last few moments are significant and offer an opportunity for you to be helpful.

Clients often feel much better after a well-conducted interview. They find it interesting to think about themselves in such detail. They learn about themselves from their disclosures. They may experience an opening of their perspective and perhaps a glimmer of potential positive change. You may follow this by contemplation to create an individualized treatment strategy. At the very least, the interview should begin to establish a sound relationship with the patient while also giving you valuable and personal information, so that your treatment will be of help.

Part Three

Carl R. Rogers Ph.D.
and
Arthur W. Combs Ph.D.

Courtesy of the Carl Rogers Memorial Library
Center for Studies of the Person

Courtesy of the Field Psych Trust
301 Dixie Street, Carrollton, Georgia 30117
Honoring the life and professional contributions
of Arthur W. Combs Ph.D.

Chapter Seven

Facilitating Growth

CARL ROGERS

Carl Rogers was a world renowned psychotherapist, famous for client-centered therapy. Although most people remember him for his approach to counseling, he devoted many years to researching his ideas as a professor-researcher at Ohio State University, University of Chicago, and University of Wisconsin. He was elected to numerous leadership positions including president of the American Psychological Association, American Association for Applied Psychology, and the American Academy of Psychotherapists. He expressed his views in his books, often using personal disclosures to communicate his ideas. Some of his best-known books are *On Becoming a Person*, *Client-Centered Therapy*, and *A Way of Being*.

Rogers' method had a broad impact on the world. Although Rogers' work was originally intended for therapists and clients, he came to view his ideas in a broader context—applying to all humanity. His client-centered vision became person-centered, applying to all humanity. He spent the later years of his life traveling around the world, guiding large groups toward a person-centered approach to life. In his direct and personal way, he encouraged people to aim for the highest potential of humanity: personal growth and fulfillment. He commented about the direction of his life, "I fall far short of achieving real communication--person-to-person--all the time, but moving in this direction makes life for me a warm, exciting, upsetting, troubling, satisfying, enriching, and above all a worthwhile venture." (Rogers & Stevens 1967, 275) His accepting, genuine way is still being taught at the Center for Studies of the Person located in La Jolla, California. Carl Rogers' approach continues to inspire.

ARTHUR COMBS

Since the very beginnings of the humanistic movement in psychology, Arthur W. Combs was unwavering in his dedication to a personal, perceptual approach to psychology. He devoted his long and productive professional life to teaching, lecturing, practice, research, and writing. He was committed to helping people understand and accept the perceptual perspective.

Dr. Combs had a distinguished career, including prominent positions on the faculty of Ohio State University, Syracuse University, University of

Florida, and the University of Northern Colorado. He founded and headed the Personal Counseling Service in Syracuse, was President of the New York State Psychological Association and Chairman of the Joint Council of New York State Psychologists. In Florida he served as Chairman of the Foundations of Education Department and the first Director of the Center for Humanistic Education. He received commendations for his research and teaching and wrote extensively, more than twenty books and numerous articles. He was exemplary in his dedication to therapy and education.

His first book, written with Donald Snygg in 1949, *Individual Behavior, A New Frame of Reference for Psychology*, was a groundbreaking work which, according to many sources, (Shaffer, 1952, Rogers, 1951, Murphy, 1949, Allport, 1949) was one of the first comprehensive statements of the humanistic perspective. His perceptual field theory has wide application. Dr. Combs' concept that personal meaning for the client must be addressed in successful treatment can enhance the work of psychotherapists today. His work is being gathered and preserved by the Field Psych Trust located in Carrollton, Georgia.

Carl Rogers Interview

We met with Carl Rogers at his home in La Jolla. He led us to a beautiful open garden area behind his house, set high up in the hills of La Jolla, California. We walked past miniature landscaping and small white stones to a group of lawn chairs, where we sat down. We could smell the sweet aromas of plants and flowers, as we looked out on a majestic view of the Pacific Ocean. It was a typically glorious sunny San Diego day. He sat comfortably, quite relaxed. He spoke to us in a friendly, warm manner, even though he was quite eminent and we were graduate students at that time. He dressed casually in a pastel colored golf shirt and slacks. He sat with one hand tipped against the side of his chin, fingers bent as we began our conversation.

We introduced ourselves and explained that we were interested in the important determiners of psychotherapeutic effectiveness. He said, "To my mind empathy is in itself one of the most potent healing agents." We recognized the parallel to Jerome Frank's concern with the therapeutic relationship as a nonspecific factor. But Frank had never specified this quality of the relationship. Rogers' idea about empathy could help to fill out this important aspect of therapeutic effectiveness.

We told him that we were students of Milton Erickson and that we were also very interested in the unconscious mind. Rogers said that he knew Dr. Erickson and was familiar with his work. We asked what thoughts he had about the unconscious. He answered, "The understanding I have of the unconscious is as an organismic awareness. I am continuing to have more and more respect for that level of functioning, below the level of consciousness.

"I believe that through congruence, unconditional positive regard, and empathy, you can tap into the unconscious. In fact, empathy is not always a conscious experience. There is a natural link between people on the unconscious level. Empathy taps into this unconscious link."

We agreed with him and recounted an experience we had with a client some years ago. The evening following a session, Annellen had a fantasy of a concentration camp. It seemed to happen out of nowhere but continued to occur to her through the week. At the next session, the client spoke about her new boyfriend. She said that he had been telling her about his experiences in a concentration camp, recounting this in great detail. Suddenly Annellen's fantasy made sense as an unconscious empathic response, her unconscious with the client's unconscious.

Rogers agreed and said, "I think this happens often when there is a good therapeutic relationship. He explained how this also relates to the natural tendency in people toward self-actualization. Self-actualization is the basic tendency for people to grow in a positive direction. He explained to us why he felt the intuitive unconscious in people is the seed of potential. "I trust people," he said decisively.

"I believe Dr. Erickson also trusted what I call the directional tendency in people, the wisdom of the organism. All people are creative in the ways they develop and grow."

We asked Rogers the same question we had asked all the psychotherapists we interviewed, "Do you believe human nature is good or bad?" Rogers' answer was consistent with his theory. He said that he believed human nature tends to the positive.

"People are essentially good. The more that we are able to be true to that intrinsic goodness within, the more the goodness is expressed." Rogers explained, "When I trust in the client's potential and step back, people tend to resolve their conflicts and become the best they can be—fulfilling their potential."

"I believe there is a formative positive tendency that counterbalances the destructiveness of entropy that science believes is the nature of things. Human beings are positive and they tend toward the positive. Not only are people positive, but the world is positive too."

"Problems come when we interfere, get in the way of the natural tendency to grow. You see that in the world of nature, all around us." Rogers enjoyed gardening, and in a sense his theory of human nature was like gardening. If we nurture the garden and give it the right conditions, it grows. But we can prevent growth by not watering, blocking the light, etc. When the conditions are wrong, people can get the idea that growth is impossible. But the small plants we see growing between the cracks in concrete are strong evidence for the natural tendency to grow!

We told him that we were studying psychotherapy deeply, hoping to evolve our own work and help others to do so as well. Rogers was known for his sensitive approach to the therapeutic relationship. The therapist brings certain human qualities to that relationship that will allow the other to grow: genuineness, empathy and unconditional positive regard. He told us that although he had devoted many years to individual therapy, he had, in recent years been moving toward working with larger and larger groups. Recently he had been to China where he helped in the facilitation of hundreds at one time. He said, "I have found that the three central qualities of genuineness, empathy, and unconditional positive regard apply in every culture. People are people around the globe. I have found this to be true wherever I go. Now that I am older, I want to use my time well. I feel I can extend this genuine caring to large groups. I feel genuine concern for humanity. It has been amazing to see people opening up and experiencing themselves differently."

We wondered whether he thought one of these qualities was more important than the others. Rogers answered, "Being genuine is the most important of all. But it's important to *really* care, not just to say you do. People have taken my theory of therapy literally. They use the techniques, such as reflecting back to the client. But if they don't genuinely care— feeling this deeply, the interaction does not touch on the truly human level, and so it becomes shallow. To touch the other person and awaken the vast inner resources within, we must genuinely care."

We have had a long-standing interest in Eastern philosophy. Rogers saw many parallels with Zen, Taoism, and Buddhism. He said, "These philosophies extend the idea of humanity outward, showing how all humanity is included in a dynamic universe. I believe that the formative tendency leads the universe toward greater complexity and interrelatedness. When we sense beyond rational consciousness to the unconscious, we also gain a transcendent awareness that includes all people. I'm hoping my group work will help to awaken these insights in all people, to help the world."

Rogers' work has deeply affected the world. He continues to be remembered. His ideas have been integrated into many forms of therapy. The quality of the therapeutic relationship and the person-to-person encounter that is therapy, have been greatly enhanced by his warmhearted open approach.

Arthur Combs Interview

We met regularly in 1970-1971 with Arthur Combs when he was teaching at the University of Florida. He was a trim man, alert and animated. He cared deeply about his country, the youth and education as well as his clients. He dedicated his life to being helpful and teaching others to be helpful. Our conversations were relaxed and open. Through our meetings he helped us understand therapy from the perceptual point of view. We conducted this interview some years later over the telephone.

Simpkins: What personal experiences brought you to your theory, leading to its personal meaning for you?

Combs: Well, it started out with my interest in trying to help kids who had problems in school. That led me to study with Carl Rogers. Carl was just beginning to develop his method of nondirective therapy, which of course was dependent upon careful listening and empathy. I had a kind of beginning point, to look at people and their behavior in that way, trying to be empathic. I finished my doctorate later after working awhile. But I was not happy about the ideas I was involved with, mostly behavioral in those days.

Then I met Donald Snygg, who was coming down to Syracuse where I was at the time, to teach an occasional course for us. One day he left me a reprint of an article he had done which was called, "The Need for a Phenomenological System in Psychology." It wasn't a very engaging title, so I stuck it into my briefcase intending to read it someday; and it stayed there for a month or two. Then I went off to New York City to give an address to the American Orthopsychiatric Association. On the way home on the train, I took out my briefcase and looked at the article he had given to me. The only way I can describe the experience is like a kind of intellectual conversion. I remember sitting on that train and thinking, "Well, what about learning, well of course! Well, what about perception, well of course! What about motivation, well of course!" and on and on like that. I remember it clearly, all kinds of questions I had just fell into place, zip, zip, zip.

I was so excited that I called Don, even though it was midnight when I got in, and asked to see him the next day. I made an appointment, went up to his office in Oswego, and said, "Don, this is the most amazing thing I've ever read. Do you know what you have done here?"

He replied, "What the hell are you talking about?" I began to show him what I saw in the framework he had presented. We sat down that afternoon and outlined *Individual Behavior*. We never changed the basic outline. We worked on it for another two years, but the major things we put down that afternoon!

The whole phenomenological point of view: the perceptual-experiential, has become a very central part of my whole life. I'm continually seeing things from this orientation, not just in the classes I teach, but also in my everyday life. It has become a very deep and fundamental part of my life.

Simpkins: Thus, your personal discovery that a theory can have a personal effect on the counselor.

Combs: What makes an effective counselor is not a question of knowledge or method; it is the belief system of the therapist. Don't worry about the methods. If you have a comprehensive theory, it deserves to be trusted. And you derive methods out of that.

Simpkins: Have you done any research on this theory?

Combs: Once we wrote the theoretical position, we did all kinds of research on various aspects of perception: The effect of threat on perception, for example. There was a study from a grant given by the US Office of Education, to map the development of self concept. We gave it up because the research people insisted we turn it into a statistical study. But it was an attempt to look at how the self concept forms as part of the educational process.

Simpkins: You didn't feel that mathematizing it as data did justice to it as a phenomenological experience?

Combs: The people who gave us the money insisted that we approach the problem as a factor analysis study. This submerged and buried what we were looking for. We found the major motivating factor was the need for adequacy. Well, that's all well and good, but what have you learned more specifically about the self concept? The individual data got lost in the attempt to make it a factor analytic study, so I gave it up.

Later we explored the difference between good helpers and bad helpers. The first study we did was with a group of counselors in training. We had them rated with respect to how effective they were in the eyes of five or six supervisors, and then we examined the question of how they perceived themselves, how they perceived their task, and what data they considered most important. We were amazed at the study because what we had were these dichotomies: sees self positively or negatively, people as friendly or unfriendly. We had about fifteen of these dichotomies, fourteen came out with significant differences, to our amazement. Good helpers were more positive on these things. Many other projects have followed up these original studies, and have shown that the difference between good helpers and bad ones is fundamentally a question of their perceptual orientation, or their belief system.

Simpkins: Did you find that this correlated with whether they were experienced or beginners or did experienced helpers of varying schools have more in common than the beginner therapists of the same school?

Combs: Yes, that's correct. Fiedler noted that long ago.

Simpkins: Most of the research on effectiveness in psychotherapy shows that all forms of therapy are similar in their effects, but there are individual differences that nobody can account for.

Combs: I think that's one of the reasons they don't get good results in some of those studies, because when you look at descriptions of what the therapist does, you're really talking about methods, and the important thing about methods is that they have to fit. And there aren't any universal ones. To really understand the dynamics of what's going on in any helping relationship, you have to deal with two variables: one is what the therapist, the teacher, or the social worker is trying to do. The other is, what does the client, or patient, think is happening. It is in that dynamic that we have to understand the process. When you look at it from an outside point of view, you are looking at it from external descriptions, which are mere expressions that come out of that dynamic, so what you are really doing is looking at symptoms. And you know you wouldn't be very happy going to a doctor who only looks at your symptoms. This is a major error that is currently being made in many places to attempt to explore what is going on in teaching situations, with social workers, therapists, or whatever. The observations that you make from an external orientation simply do not hold up.

Simpkins: This is one of the interesting aspects of your theory, that you are able to be inbetween. You felt that a totally internal point of view could miss the point, without the interaction. Some phenomenologists are so abstract in their subjectivity that they aren't really talking about anything that anybody would understand. And the same for some behaviorists.

Combs: What Don and I have offered here is the early stages of a whole psychology of meaning, which I think for me is absolutely essential on which to ground the Humanistic Movement.

Simpkins: There is a reawakening of interest in Earl Kelley's concepts and transformation of meaning. Jerome Frank defines psychotherapy as a transformation of meaning.

Combs: It seems to me that education and therapy are helping people to discover personal meaning. This is the particular theoretical position that makes it possible for us to talk about these things in ways that can be ordered for research purposes. Unfortunately, most of what is going on in humanistic psychology is philosophical, which precludes any disciplined observation.

Simpkins: Could you enlarge on what you mean by meaning?

Combs: I've never tried to define it. It is what the brain is trying to do. Brain researchers tell us that what the brain is trying to do is make meaning out of experience. I would say that meaning means to make sense. Meaning is the personal perception of the relationship, to himself, that the person has with events. We are constantly in the process of trying to make meaning out of experience, to make sense out of experience, so that it can be utilized, sorted out, differentiated between what is important and what is not.

Simpkins: People discover meaning through their interaction with the world and their experience. We have understood Rogers to imply that the organism should have a consistency between the self concept and the actual self. An inaccurate self-image throws off self-actualization. Consistency of meaning is an important criterion of health and what you try to bring about in therapy. Are we correct in assuming that?

Combs: I'd agree with this. Meaning is everything; it is what it is all about. Pathology comes about as a result of distorted meanings and inconsistencies.

Each of us operates on an internal belief system. We get into difficulties when that belief system has within it internal incongruities. I believe this but I also believe that and then I realize, my God, I can't believe both of those things at the same time. One of the things that the therapist tries to do is help the client weed out those inconsistencies and distorted meanings, to develop a smoother, fuller, more internally consistent belief about himself and the world which makes it possible for him to behave with maximum freedom and maximum efficiency also.

Simpkins: How do emotions fit into that?

Combs: Emotion is a theoretical position; it is a mere artifact. Any behavior has more or less of a degree of acceleration that goes along with it with respect to body processes. And that is what produces what people call emotion. When a dog is snapping at me and my palms get wet and my blood pressure goes up and I get ready to flee or fight, this we call emotion. But it is merely an artifact of what goes along with the perception of meaning.

Simpkins: So you view the belief system as prior and the emotional reaction comes from that?

Combs: Sure, and the closer an event comes to the self, the greater is the degree of emotion that is experienced. I use the example of the woman who has a lover overseas and he is coming home in six months. No big deal. He's coming home in one month, one week, one day, he's on his way, here comes his plane, there he is. As the event becomes closer, the degree of emotion becomes higher and higher. The amount of emotion experienced is a function of the reference to self.

Simpkins: In your books and papers you used the self and the self-concept interchangeably. Are they the same thing? Or is the concept how the person construes himself?

Combs: Phenomenologically, they are the same thing. The only thing I know is what I think about myself, know about myself. What other people tell me is external. It's something I have to react to. For example, if somebody says to me, Combs, that was pretty stupid; I have to react to that and deal with it.

   What I am trying to do in therapy is help people explore and discover better ways to see themselves and the world. In the process of doing that, they have to look at their relationships with the world. They have to do it because they are living in the world. There is a saying, "All roads lead to Rome". Wherever you start, you'll get there. Because if a person is really growing more healthy and exploring himself, he's got to confront his problem areas, because his fundamental need is to maintain and enhance himself. And if he can, he will. He must explore the things he needs to explore.

Simpkins: Do you have a case illustrating the denial of inconsistency and its importance?

Combs: Mrs. Jones comes to see me and says, "My husband is a heel and a brute", and off she goes down the road. "He did this, and he did that, and he did that."

   I'm responding to how she's feeling about that. I'm ignoring what she's saying and responding to her feeling about that. I say, "I can see you feel kind of violated by him."

And she says, "Yes I do!" And she goes off about it. So I say, "I can see that you feel very angry about him."

"I do." And off she goes again. After a while, she stops, and says, "One thing I can say for him is that he has a bunch of friends and they just think he's the greatest thing on earth. But not me." And away we go again.

So I continue to respond to her feelings and help her to clarify them and hold them up for her to look at. Then she stops and says, "Well one thing I can say for him is that he has never forgotten my birthday. But...then..." away we go again. "But you know", she stops and says, "You know, I have to admit, that maybe part of this is me." And then we are off on another track. But here is the change, when she came in she said, "He's a heel and a brute, no doubt about it." Then she says, "Not everybody thinks so", then she says, "Not even I always think so". And then she says, "Dr. Combs, you can't change him, but maybe I can change, and I'd like to come back again." This is how the perceptions change in the process of therapy. She comes finally to look at the situation with a closer respect for reality.

Each of us lives in the culture. We have to live in the culture. So if we create a therapeutic situation that helps the person come more in touch with the culture, you've got to come face to face with the discrepancy.

Simpkins: You see your role as facilitating but not standing in judgment over what is a good or bad adjustment?

Combs: This is what I have against confrontation. You break the relationship with the client. If I confront you, I've taken the power and it is no longer a cooperative, facilitative relationship. That's one thing. The other thing is that my experience with confrontation, until the person is ready to confront something, is that it simply delays the process, because what happens when a person is confronted? They become threatened. Then they are forced to defend their existing position. So I don't call what I do confrontation. I may suggest something, but a suggestion can be rejected. They always have a choice. For example, in the first interview, I would never say, "Well that's a stupid thing to do". But later on, when the relationship between client and therapist is so open and trusting, I can say, "Well, that was kind of a stupid thing to do". And the client might say, "Yeah it was", or he might say, "You're crazy, Combs". He could argue with me. But in the first interview, he can't argue with you, because you are in the position of power; not until he finds out that you don't have the power, and that this is truly a facilitative relationship. When you reach this, you can make suggestions. They are accepted as data, rather than as oughts or shoulds.

Simpkins: So you define the role as facilitative, and stick to this position always.

Combs: Yes, I'm a facilitator or a helper.

Simpkins: Does this tend to only work in a counseling setting rather than a psychiatric or psychotherapeutic situation?

Combs: No. I have used it with hospitalized psychiatric patients and so did Carl Rogers. The same dynamics hold for psychotics, neurotics, ordinary Joes, and even for the learning process. It's just a question of degree of distortion that is involved. That's not to say that there may not also be physiological factors. Those aren't my business because I'm not a physician.

The organism is moving toward the maintenance and enhancement of self: self-actualization. Threat is an aberration along the way that causes distortion and causes people to be unable to see clearly, to perceive with accuracy, leading to tunnel vision, and the need to defend the self.

As far as I'm concerned, the therapeutic process is an outgrowth of the therapist's belief system, and interacting with the client with concern for how things seem to the client, to try to help him sort out his perceptions and come to new and better ones.

Simpkins: How do you get the sense of the inner dynamics of the person? Because you don't use a theory of personality per se, but rather the perceptual field.

Combs: This involves empathy. All of us do this automatically. Young children are deeply sensitive to what is felt by their mothers and dads. For them it's a matter of survival. What happens is that as we grow up, all of us are sensitive to what other people are thinking and feeling. The difficulty is that as we grow older, we don't do it with the people we don't have to. For example, I'm sure that you are deeply sensitive to your wife's feelings, and you modify your feelings accordingly. Each of us is deeply sensitive to those people whose feelings are important to us. But we forget to be empathic with people who aren't important to us. And the whole society does this. Now, what this means is that the business of understanding how things seem to other people is not something we have to learn. We all know how to do it. We have to learn to do it more effectively, more systematically, and more often.

Simpkins: So how would you go about training a person to do this? How would you bring this out, and help them return to it?

Combs: You help people to be empathic by teaching them where to look. If it is true that behavior is a function of perception, then we have to train people to observe behavior and infer the perception that produced it. You keep doing that over a period of time, and you refine and refine until you're pretty accurate, right on the nose, really thinking and feeling. It's a process of inference that you use.

Simpkins: There seems to be an assumption that nobody can understand a problem or role they have not personally experienced.

Combs: Yes, but you can come pretty close if you make the effort. When you talk of feelings, you are trying to describe the state of your phenomenal field at this moment. When you say, I'm angry with Mr. Jones, you are saying that that's the meaning of the situation you are confronting at this point. Carl Rogers in his original psychotherapy had a technique called recognition and acceptance of feeling. In my language you could just as easily have said recognition and acceptance of personal meaning. Because when you talk about your feeling, that is really a shorthand description of your phenomenal field. The phenomenal field is made up of meaning. It is your field of meaning.

To put it in a nutshell, what I'm trying to do is construct a theory of therapy that is consistent with a larger theory of psychology. Therapy must come out of a fundamental theory of meaning from psychology. I want to be able to support anything I do, as a therapist, with some kind of consistent, internally congruent system. For me eclecticism is an anathema. I'm trying to develop a whole theory of psychology and then develop a theory of therapy that would grow out of it for the larger psychological discipline.

The concepts Combs taught are now an accepted part of humanistic therapy and education. His commitment to self-actualization and understanding personal meanings of clients inspired our direction when we began to learn psychotherapy more than thirty years ago. And he is still inspiring today.

If behavior is the product of perception, the limits of human potentiality are restricted only by the richness, extent, and availability of perceptions in a person's personal field of meaning. The eventual possibilities for human beings in such a view of human potential are beyond comprehension.

Arthur W. Combs

An empathic way of being can be learned from empathic persons. Perhaps the most important statement of all is that the ability to be accurately empathic is something that can be developed by training... Empathy is clearly related to positive outcome.

Carl R. Rogers

PART THREE

Chapter Eight

The Meaning of Fulfillment

What you strive for is within you, seek it not
without.   (Persius)

PERSONAL MEANING
The perceptual approach is the starting point for theory. Rogers and
Combs set personal meaning in the center of their theory. They did not
believe in basing therapy on either external approaches, such as
behaviorism's direct observation of behavior, or internal approaches, such
as phenomenological focus on experience. A wider frame of reference is
needed that includes both. The perceptual process is essential for empirical
reality to have effects. Behavior must be perceived to be observed. But
behavior must take place for the perceptual process to manifest: something
must be perceived. Both are included when observed from the perceptual
point of view.
The present is the vantage point from which perception takes place.
The past is of significance during therapy as a function of the present. The
perception that people have at the moment of action: their personally
meaningful experiencing, leads to behavior.

BEHAVIOR AND PERSONAL MEANING
People behave according to how things seem to them. As Combs said
succinctly, "An individual's behavior is understood to be a direct
consequence of the total field of personal meanings existing at that instant,
the individual perceptual field" (Combs, Avila, Purkey 1978, 19). Perception
of personal meaning is the primary data of therapy, and therefore change
in personal meaning is the essence of therapeutic change. Awareness of
the client's perceptions, thoughts, and feelings is fundamental. Combs in
explaining his theory said that the brain is a marvelous organ for perceiving
meaning. All perception is meaningful. So behavior does not occur in a
vacuum. And responses do not come directly from stimuli. Behavior is a
function of personal meaning. The meaning of the stimulus and its

consequences to the person is what people respond to; and the response is a product of the total perceptual field. The perceptual field perspective leads to certain consequences in behavior.

Otto Rank (1884-1939) was one of the earliest psychotherapists to introduce the internal orientation. He believed that the search for actual truth about psychic matters in relation to the past, or even to the present, is not what therapy is. Historical documents are only memory. Therapeutically, searching for true facts in the past is unnecessary. Clients often live better with their own conception of things than in the knowledge of the actual fact. Most importantly, Rank believed that only the inner past determines the present ego. Therapists can only understand the actual events when they understand the individual's attitude toward them. (Rank, 1978) This points us toward perception

The perceptual point of view holds that the client's conception is the client's fact. The early founders of the construct of intelligence in psychology recognized this position. Alfred Binet, original creator of intelligence testing, wrote:

> ...We can suggest that sensation is something formless which we cannot even describe in words, and that its precision and significance are produced by the interpretation which we give it. Thus, due to this intellectual alluvium, a sensation produced by the same stimulus varies profoundly from one person to another, receiving the imprint of each personality... In external perception, the external force does not dominate us; rather, it is we—our intelligence—who dominate it. (Binet, Selected Papers, 73)

So we don't just receive through the senses. Our interpretation is an integral part of sensing. Objective reality is actually a function of our minds.

FIELD THEORY

Perception is primary. Combs' field theory offered this paradigm to shift the focus for therapy from external to internal. Each person has a unique perceptual field. The resulting experience is meaningful, consistent and lawful. "The perceptual field is the entire universe, including himself, as it is experienced by an individual at the instant of action" (Combs, Richards, Richards 1976, 22).

Field theory is a method of analyzing causal relations and building scientific constructs. The field theory developed in physics brought this general way of conceptualizing into the spotlight as important for understanding phenomena. When field theory is adapted to psychology, it permits concepts from such varied positions as Gestalt, holism and self-actualization to meld together in a meaningful synthesis. Previously, strict behavioral theory assumed that a reflex response inside the organism was elicited directly from a stimulus outside the organism. This process was known as the reflex arc. But field theory proposes a field of interaction through the perceptual process. The arc is a circle. Stimulus and response, organism and environment are all needed for each to take place. Existing in a field, each is related to the others.

Therefore, unity within the perceived situation must be the starting point for psychological theory, according to Lewin, an early proponent of field theory in psychology. He stated, "Only by the concrete whole which comprises the object and the situation are the vectors that determine the dynamics of the event defined" (Cartwright in Koch 1959, 17).

The client's behavior is determined by the client's perception of the situation. The source of response is what the stimulus seems to be to the client: Its personal meaning. The field of meaning as a whole must be the focus. The foundation of theory must rest there, not on presumed causes from learning, memory, or other processes.

Lewin's Constructive Field Theory

Lewin formalized his position on field theory while still remaining linked to empirical experimentation. His field theory addressed dynamic interrelationships that became the interdependence of parts within the whole field. His theory was groundbreaking and ahead of its time.

Lewin distinguished between what he called Aristotelian and Galilean modes of thought. Aristotelian, or closed systems, are based on the classical scientific method of abstraction. Experimenters observe what are considered objective phenomena and select out a certain feature believed to be held in common with other similar situations. Then they proceed from the particular feature to the universal principle, through inductive reasoning. But the vertical lattice of abstract reasoning in search of the ideal can evolve farther and farther away from the real world. This may result in a statistical scheme that is untrue to the actual individual case. Closed system logic may not always return to the empirical world of sensible experience.

Closed systems have an important place in theorizing, but it is a mistake to try to use this approach exclusively to determine therapy procedures or evaluate results. Instead, Lewin proposed the Galilean method. He aimed to discover connections among the laws that govern each field of experience, by proceeding from the life space, or field, as a whole.

The Galilean method of theory construction relates a network of interacting constructs in horizontal or lateral relationship, rather than in a vertical hierarchy. One construct alone is only a part, and does not embody the whole, the essence of the theory. Since any construct is only an individual part, it can be subtracted or unplugged from the network, if found unnecessary or incorrect, without jeopardizing the whole theory. If the theory as a whole is correct, the actual behavior of the person in the life situation should be explainable. "What is real is what has effects." (Lewin 1936, 19) This extends the experimental paradigm by using reasoning in an open, flexible way.

In keeping with this emphasis, rather than search for features and then abstract principles or concepts that classify, Lewin encouraged researchers to use fundamental constructs. From these one can explain and predict likely events and unlikely events. Hypotheses can be derived from the expected relationships among the constructs, which should be internally consistent. Hypotheses can be tested empirically using standard experimental methods and procedures. Individual constructs can be explored for their validity. Then, by successive approximation, a correct theory takes form. This permits better prediction than other methods, along with continual improvement.

When the Aristotelian method is used in psychology an event or effect is derived from its cause, usually the causal nature of a single fact, attribute, or faculty such as personality, drive, or emotion. By contrast, the Galilean method involves the thesis: an event or effect is always the result of relationship, the interaction of several causes. A psychological event involves the dynamic interaction of multiple variables. For example, with regard to the traditional question of whether nature or nurture is the chief determiner of behavior, field theorists propose that an interaction is the more valid way to view it: Individual features are meaningful in terms of the whole. Both Aristotelian and Gallilean methods can be useful.

In order to predict and understand behavior, study the total individual field. Do not abstract and standardize individual features and then attempt to derive predictions of behavior. They lose their significance when taken out of context. The domain of determinism is within each individual field of interaction. Therefore each case is self-consistent, determined and lawful, if viewed in relationship to its context: the individual perceptual field. Field theory can help to develop the basis for a comprehensive approach for psychotherapy without being at odds with determinism, which is necessary for a science of the person. This is how an individual's perceptual field, when truly known, permits prediction of behavior. Practitioners must begin with the self-concept.

SELF-CONCEPT

The center of the universe for the individual of
necessity is their self-concept. (Combs 1976, 160)

The phenomenal self is at the center of the perceptual field, which includes perceptions of both self and world. The perceptual field is not identical with the objective or physical field, though it interacts. The "self concept" means those aspects of people's perceptual fields that they refer to when they say "I" or "Me": all the thousands of perceptions, beliefs and ideas about the self that go to make up the individual, such as who we are, what we do, where we live, and what we are like. It includes concepts of self in relationship, such as "I am a writer, I am a psychologist," and so on. Self concept is not identical with the physical or biological self, though it may overlap--it goes beyond the skin or body. The self-concept does not have to be a Western one. For example, the Eastern self-concept is not to be an individual, apart and isolated from others or the world, but instead, the self includes them. For Zen Buddhists, concept of self is not conceptualized. They focus on experience. So concepts of self may take very different forms.

But though there are many individual perceptions of it, the self is unitary. The therapist's task is to facilitate clients to change their self-concept toward more satisfying and fulfilling self-definitions. This requires attempting to understand the situation from the client's point of view, and direct all therapeutic efforts to the situation, as the client perceives it.

The self of any human being always tends towards self-actualization, which means to enhance and maintain itself. Self-actualization will push the human being towards enhancement: better functioning, a higher synthesis of being, the best one can be; in other words fulfillment. The self-concept tends to stabilize and orient behavior in each individual life.

> The self-concept lies at the very center of a person's existence, one's most precious possession. On the one hand it must be cherished, protected, and defended; on the other, it must be constantly buttressed, embellished, and enriched. This is not easy to accomplish in modern complex societies. (Combs 1989, 49)

These counterbalances in the personality lead to a dynamic equilibrium, which energizes and pushes towards change and positive striving while preserving and maintaining the individual's integrity and stability.

CHANGE AND THE SELF CONCEPT

Sometimes the self-concept needs to change with the demands of new experiences, times, and places. The self-concept must be fixed enough for some sense of stability but flexible enough to respond. It needs to change and shift when situations require. If change is not allowed, disharmony results. For example, when the self-concept is too rigid, situations requiring individuals to act in ways beyond the limits of their self-concept may be perceived as threatening. The individual is faced with several choices: avoid the situation or act inconsistently with the self-concept. Healthy individuals will eventually respond by altering their self-concept. The experience of threat affects the phenomenal self, through the concept of self. In healthy functioning, the self-concept is continually growing and developing. Self-concepts must be consistent. Threat leads away from openness.

Therapy requires loosening of defensiveness and rigid boundaries leading to disorganization and reorganization of the self-concept. This affects the perceptual field. A new configuration gradually emerges which includes previously denied, unrecognized or rejected aspects of self and others. An enhanced perceptual field gradually emerges in therapy, including more, as the person engages in the continuous process of becoming whole.

HOMEOSTASIS AND BEYOND

Most psychodynamic formulations are based in a concept of homeostasis. Homeostasis has a long and distinguished history in the literature. Claude Bernard in his classic *The Experimental Study of Medicine* developed the concept while establishing rigorous experimentation in medicine. He demonstrated that there is a stable internal milieu that the body prefers and returns to whenever possible. An example is body temperature, for most people 98.6 degrees.

Cannon developed the concept further (Cannon, 1963) and pointed to social implications. He viewed the human organism as striving for balance, equilibrium, and stability. The natural stable milieu of living is positive, not just negative. For example, body temperature does not tend either to be too hot or too cold.

Adaptation to circumstances includes both plus and minus directions. This became an important part of stress theory. Psychodynamic theory assumes the importance of balance in the psychological realm, not just the physical. The organism's psychological balance is disturbed by tension from unsatisfied needs. When needs are satisfied, tension is relieved, and balance is restored. Many psychodynamic formulations are based in this assumption, taking its truth for granted.

But Combs viewed tension-reduction as only a partial explanation. Motivation is not just from a deficit. The apparently multi-varied needs experienced by the individual are really part of the process of pursuing the master need: self-actualization. This is the fundamental need, according to Combs. All basic needs are forms of the deeper need for self-actualization.

SELF-ACTUALIZATION

The self of any human being always tends towards self-actualization, which means to enhance and maintain itself. Self-actualization will push the human being towards enhancement: better functioning, a higher synthesis of being, the best one can be; in other words fulfillment. The human organism tends to work as a whole, to seek for the best possible level of organized functioning. The person is part of the universe, and the universe is itself striving, in a sense, for more organization and wholeness, expressed in terms of the human beings within it as well. This is a positive and counterbalancing tendency to the somewhat negative well-known law of thermodynamics that the universe tends towards disorder and chaos. Humanity is a positive force in the world. The universe is evolving. There is hope and reason to be optimistic.

Self-actualization involves a search for personal adequacy and integrity. All healthy personality moves towards self-actualization, to fulfill each individual's destiny. Only unhealthy personality moves away from it. Thus, for example, delinquents are essentially unfulfilled, deprived people, whose self-concepts tend to maintain them in their identity. Lower levels of personal adequacy are expressed in this way, partly due to lack of self-acceptance. There is a logical implication to self-actualization: negative behavior is a less adequate response to a perceived threat. Since the threatened person is not as open and self-accepting, reactions based on distorted information and perceptions of self come about. Therapy should restore the person to positive striving for fulfillment. This becomes possible through empathy.

EMPATHY

Empathy is one of the most delicate and powerful
ways we have of using ourselves. (Rogers 1980, 137)

Sincere empathy is basic to good counseling. Seeing the situation from the client's point of view permits a better understanding of the meaning. According to Rogers, empathy is one of our best tools for understanding personality dynamics and affecting changes in personality and behavior.

Rogers defined empathy as a process where the therapist enters the private perceptual world of the other. "It involves being sensitive, moment to moment, to the changing felt meanings that flow in the other person, to the fear or rage or tenderness or confusion or whatever that he or she is experiencing" (Rogers 1980, 142).

Both Rogers and Combs stressed repeatedly that the best way to understand people is from their own frame of reference, the one internal to their own perceptual field. The client's frame of reference can be inferred by observing behaviors and expressed feelings, leading to empathy.

Over the years the research evidence has kept piling up, and it points strongly to the conclusion that a high degree of empathy in a relationship is possibly the most important factor in bringing about change and learning. (Rogers 1980, 139)

Many researchers have recognized the importance of empathy. Empathy is an important factor in therapeutic effectiveness. (Raskin, 1974)

From analysis of eighty-three practicing therapists with eight different therapeutic approaches, Raskin concluded that one of the most important factors is "trying as sensitively and accurately as one can, to understand the client from the latter's own point of view." (Raskin, 1974) A number of studies found that the more experienced the therapist, the more likely that he or she is skilled in empathy. (Fiedler 1950, Mullen & Abeles 1972.)

The English word "empathy" is similar to the German word "einfuhlung" which means "feeling into." A natural empathetic response occurs in everyday life. Spectators watching a high jumper will lean forward as the jumper takes off. This tendency to "feel into" the action of another taps into a similar mechanism to the ideomotor phenomenon. For example, imagine a tart lemon and your mouth will begin to salivate automatically. This is a natural response that occurs without thought. Therapists can empathically link their own ideo-responses to those of the client. This permits the practitioner to understand the client's perspective. When this happens, therapists will not judge mystifying behavior quite as strange and bizarre, and as a result can help their clients discover more effective and adaptive responses to their situation.

Combs once interviewed a man who was picked up by the police and confined to a mental hospital because he was found walking the streets of New York with no clothes on. Hospital intake records reported: "Patient shows high levels of depression and anxiety. Reason for admission: irrational behavior, walking streets nude."

Here is what the patient reported about his dilemma: "I've had these terrible fears ever since I got out of the army. Lately they got so bad I checked myself in at the hospital. They kept me four days and told me I was all right, that I was just having an anxiety attack. Things didn't get better. They got worse, so I went back to the hospital but they wouldn't take me in. A bartender friend said,

"If I was you, I'd make them take me in." So, I went out in the street, took off my clothes and started to walk to the hospital. But the cops picked me up before I got there." Irrational behavior? Not from the patient's point of view! (Combs 1989, 34)

The patient needed treatment, so he performed a desperate but harmless action that got him the attention he needed. After the therapist understood, better alternatives could be pointed out.

Empathy is an invaluable instrument for monitoring and feedback, to evaluate how the client is responding to the therapy. Accurate empathy allows the perspective of the client to become clear. Without empathy, behavior may make little sense and perhaps give an inaccurate meaning to observers: Some of the qualities which the therapist must develop in order to become more empathic are sensitivity, listening skills, knowing what to listen for, observation skills, using the self as instrument, and most important, the willingness and desire to be empathetic. Training in these skills will be given in Chapter 9.

THERAPEUTIC RELATIONSHIP

The helping atmosphere can make a difference in therapeutic outcome. Extensive research confirms its central importance. (Frank & Frank, 1991) In order to learn how to help his clients in the best possible way, Rogers studied the process of psychotherapy for many years. He formulated the view that it was not the school of thought of the therapist, or the techniques that actually bring about change. Instead, effective therapists share certain therapeutic attitudes: genuineness, empathy, and unconditional positive regard for the client.

Warmth, caring, and prizing of the client are primary ingredients in the therapeutic relationship, essential to understanding the client from his or her own point of view. Therapeutic warmth, a kind of pure primitive energy, is communicated through feelings rather than intellect. Shared warmth facilitates the therapeutic process. Rogers called this "non-possessive warmth" (Rogers & Stevens, 1967) that he believed communicated acceptance, caring and an invitation to relate emotionally to the client. Rogers also believed the therapist needs to genuinely care and feel positive emotionally, not just radiate hollow, unfeeling acceptance based on intellectual understanding. This concept has been important to all the psychotherapists included in this book. Frank's research showed therapeutic relationship an important nonspecific factor in effective psychotherapy.

Therefore, the counselor needs to genuinely care as a professional about what the client means by feelings, reactions, and experiences explored in therapy. Techniques do not substitute and are not therapeutic if insincere.

Rogers believed that since meaningful perception comes about through direct experience, the therapist should not define or describe the relationship to the client. Leave it open to experience instead.

The therapeutic relationship must reduce threat and provide safety, protection, and acceptance. Therapy becomes possible when the usual ways of organizing the perceptual field no longer meet the person's needs; or discrepancies, inadequacies and inconsistencies multiply to become problematic. Unconditional acceptance by the therapist of the client helps to bring neglected attributes of the client's personality to awareness for therapeutic work. In the safety of the relationship, change becomes possible. But other influences can obstruct the process.

THREAT AND LEARNING

Learning is helped or hindered by challenge or threat. According to Whitehorn, challenge has great value in personality development (Whitehorn, 1953). People may improve their performance in order to cope with adversity on their path. But on the other hand, according to

Combs, too much challenge may become threatening, which reduces potential to learn and adapt. People are "turned on" by challenge but "turned off" by threat. They become more concerned with self-defense than with change when they feel threatened. The need for self-actualization causes attention to be focused on the threatening object or situation for self-maintenance, resulting in tunnel vision. Tunnel vision can also be evoked by positive experiences as well, such as in love, when all the attention is focused on the loved one to the exclusion of everything else.

Psychological distress is a direct consequence of threat that cannot be adequately coped with. Threat may teach someone not to do something but it does not teach why or offer creative alternatives. Naturally, there is a perceptual aspect: threat depends on how a situation is perceived and what it means. One person may find a situation threatening that another does not, due to the perception of themselves as inadequate to cope with the task. Then threat may be dealt with by denial or selective editing. Skilled therapists are able to lessen threat, improving therapeutic effectiveness. Therapy needs to address this perceptual experience. Learning is reduced under threat to maintenance of self and thus is likely to be narrower in scope.

For example, delinquent children may not think that rules apply to them, since they want to do something against the regulations. The rules have a different personal meaning for delinquent children than for well-behaved children. When children who are usually well behaved do something bad they may revise their self-concept to include that sometimes they makes mistakes or misbehave, as most humans do occasionally. They can expand their self concept without feeling threatened. When interpreted differently, threat becomes challenge. For successful coping, children need to develop a self-concept of adequacy.

Sometimes due to meeting and resolving challenges life may be perceived in more positive ways, opening new potentials for being. Following the positive experience of expending great effort in a task, people sometimes discover that their energy and enthusiasm reach a new plateau, another level of potential rather than just exhaustion. An invigorating feeling of vitality is gained that is a plus rather than a minus, as stress theory would expect. This may be why we seek such experiences, rather than avoid them. They are beneficial to us.

When there is a need to learn, learning is facilitated. For example, a hungry rat will learn a maze faster than a rat that is not hungry, when food is the reward. Increasing the strength of the subject's need may accelerate the rate of learning. (Combs & Richards 1976, 198) Necessity is the mother of invention. But threat interferes with the need to learn, by emphasizing the organism's need for self-preservation at the expense of personal enhancement.

Threat can become challenge, depending upon one's personal interpretation of it. There are always a multitude of examples of both types of reaction during natural disasters. Some people become heroes, others fall apart. Similar to children, adults will cope more successfully when they develop a perception of the self as adequate. The individual's perceptual field influences learning and reaction to threat.

AUTHENTICITY

Authenticity lies at the very heart of the counseling process (Combs 1989, 157).

The client's perceived meanings should unite as a whole. This is affected profoundly by the open or closed quality of the person's awareness, which either permits or obstructs corrective feedback. Therapy helps clients be more open. Even strictly behaviorally oriented methods can be used to give feedback that may paradoxically enhance self-awareness.

If clients are not open to the meaning of actual inner experiencing, they may be misled by inappropriate concepts or ideas that have been improperly internalized and used for orientation. Therapy is directed at restoring the person to wholeness, unity and integrity, through the discovery and exploration of personal meanings.

Rogers (Rogers & Stevens 1967, 20) believed that the inner organism has intuitive wisdom through its self actualization process. He also believed this could help solve value conflicts: Values need not be imposed; they are already inherently part of normal, healthy functioning. Fully self-actualizing persons are models for values that all should strive for. Disharmony with true inner nature leads to unhealthy or bad behavior. Authenticity, analogous to honesty, reflects this as an accurate fit between concept and experience, ideas and feeling, thought and action. The past and the anticipated future play an important part of the sequence. Therefore, therapy begins with returning clients to accurate contact with their inner experience. The therapist directs clients' attention to their true feelings, and encourages clients to describe them, contemplate the meaning, and then choose action that accords with fulfillment of positive values, actualizing the true self.

THEORY AND ITS TRANSCENDENCE

Combs believed that what makes therapies effective is what they have in common. Over time therapists tend to be more similar in what they actually do, regardless of their publicly avowed theory to account for it. The publicly held theory is often at odds with what therapists privately really feel and do with patients. Combs believed that privately held theories have more to do with how therapists conduct therapy than their publicly held theoretical commitments. Therefore it makes sense to choose a theory responsibly and continue to refine it, with careful attention to research on its effectiveness, since it will become so much a part of the practice.

> The value of a theoretical position lies in the fact that it provides a frame of reference for effective use of the self as an instrument in the therapeutic process. (Combs 1989, 63)

The beliefs people have about themselves are constantly present, fundamental in determining actions. Therefore people in the helping professions must understand and use their system of beliefs to beneficially influence their clients.

Appreciating the uniqueness and differences in clients leads to less conflict with clients. Tolerant and accepting attitudes and beliefs can affect clients positively, since expectations affect the client's progress. The experienced therapist's views tend to move in the direction of less and less advice. Only clients have full access to their own perceptual field, so they should choose. The therapist encourages the client in actualizing the true self rather than actualizing a self-concept that is more distantly related to the self. Then the growth process does the rest, through the natural drive toward self actualization, the source of change.

TECHNIQUE

Initially Rogers developed powerful techniques of reflecting feeling. Rogers was persuasive and detailed in his descriptions and research, which led to a flood of studies and technology for replication. But when people merely imitated the techniques that he had worked out for himself, the techniques became only a hollow shell with little meaning. They were not using their own meanings from the source. The deeper essence, a therapeutic relationship with a warm, caring, empathic therapist, was disregarded. (Rogers, 1980)

In the years following his papers on technique and research of their parameters, Rogers emphasized relationship variables and philosophical presuppositions, partly to counterbalance this. Combs and other humanistic therapists continued in this tradition, which was in accord with their findings about what worked best. The nondirective approach, as Rogers meant it, was never intended to be mechanistic. The moment-to-moment therapeutic interaction with the client is the best source of technique.

> No particular technique per se brings about change. The probability of therapeutic movement in a particular case depends primarily not upon the counselor's personality, nor upon his techniques, nor even upon his attitudes, but upon the way all these are experienced by the client in the relationship. (Rogers & Stevens, 1967)

Techniques convey meanings. Different techniques and even different methods may convey the same meaning, depending on how the intention of the therapist is experienced and perceived through the meaning world of the client. The same technique, used in a different way, can communicate a different meaning. A smile in response to a depressed client's disclosures could mean to the client that the therapist is feeling warm and kindly or that the therapist does not take the client seriously. No one meaning is *the* meaning. Experiment with various techniques. There are no intrinsically "right" ones. Standardized meaning, perfection of form, and ease of imitation should not be the criterion for adopting a technique. The belief systems of the therapist and client are primary. Each is unique. So the criterion should be whether the technique can be used to apply the therapist's own personal theory of interaction.

A new potential for behavior should develop which cannot be explained by the elements that constitute it. This is creative learning. Imitation of another's behavior misses the point entirely. From the context of personal meaning, change is the central issue. Behavior is transformed through change in its meaning.

CONCLUSION

Learning is a personal experience: the discovery of personal meaning. For the clinical situation, objective truth is of less importance. The truth is in its usefulness for the client. All therapy material should be understood as much as possible from the client's point of view, the perceptual field. In therapy, the subjective truth matters more: how does the individual experience it? The criterion is the fit with the individual's perceptual field. When persons are understood from their own point of view, the therapist is freed to help clarify meaning. Then the client will tend to search for more adequate and fulfilling behavior.

Timeless Teachings

Chapter Nine

Enhancing Therapeutic Sensitivities

DEVELOPMENT OF EMPATHY

Empathy is a basic communication on the emotional level between client and therapist: Developing sensitivity can enhance capacity to empathize. Practitioners should sensitize themselves to emotional experience by seeking out broadening experiences in areas such as visual arts, sculpture, literature, music, and so on, to appreciate and feel reactions. By learning to be less defensive, you can facilitate your empathic reactions.

SENSITIVITY: EXERCISE IN EXPERIENCING EMOTION

Listen to good music for the emotional response you feel. Do not analyze its patterns. Just let it evoke feelings. Classical, especially if you enjoy this type of music, is the traditional method. But if classical music does not speak to you, listen to a form of music that you enjoy and feel response to. The important quality of the music is its personal meaning. Allow yourself to be immersed in the experience. Take note of your feelings and their meaning to you. The same may be done with other arts. Through music, art, literature, theater, and movies, you can have experiences on the emotional level, to learn about yourself in the process. Experience and note your feelings first. Perhaps later, trace how the meaning was related.

Learning to be empathic does not require learning something new. All people have the capacity to empathize with others, especially those they care about. Most people do not utilize their natural skills often enough. Therapists need to rediscover their own ability. Frequent use helps. The process can be broken down into two parts: observation and inference.

OBSERVATION

The capacity to observe is something we are all born with, but it can be surprising how little most people actually use it. You can practice observation and sharpen your skills. The following exercises are designed to help you develop your natural, inborn powers of observation.

OBSERVATION ENHANCEMENT

Pick a simple household object, one that you use frequently such as a kitchen utensil or a tool. Place it several feet away from you. Now observe this object carefully for several minutes. Notice its color, shape, and all of its aspects. You may be surprised to discover details about the object that you never noticed before.

Next, close your eyes and picture the object. Try to include all the details in your picture. Open your eyes and look at the object again. Did you include everything in your image? How do you feel about it? How do you feel about engaging in this exercise? What personal meanings of this object have you experienced? What does it mean to you? What might it mean to another? Can you describe these meanings in words? This exercise can be creatively varied in many ways.

INFERRING PERCEPTUAL FIELDS FROM OBSERVATION

The inner life of the client is the focal point for observation. This has been interpreted in various ways, as shown throughout the theory sections of this text: dynamics, motivations, and perceptual field are just a few. People tell the therapist many things about themselves: their feelings, attitudes, and ways of seeing things. The therapist infers from the client's statements and behaviors what is important to facilitate therapy. You can begin to train in inference by sharpening your observation skills.

Observe people in varied settings such as grocery stores, art galleries, shopping malls to learn about their perceptual fields. Notice details about their behavior, movements, ways of talking, emotional tone, attitudes, etc. People can be fascinating to observe.

READING BEHAVIOR BACKWARDS

Behavior derives from the inner experiences, perceptions, and dynamics of the individual. Clients tell us a great deal about themselves, but their information may lead therapists away from the real source of the difficulty. Learn to reason backwards from clients' behavior in their life situations, so that you can understand the pattern of their inner world. Then you may help your clients discover even better ways of behaving in accord.

Use the perceptual field concept in your own personal way, which is what Combs intended. Combine skills in observation and empathy with inference through your feeling and intuition. You can learn to use all that you are and experience to benefit your client. Study behavior in all of the circumstances you find yourself in.

Ask yourself the following question: How would your client have to feel or believe, to behave this way? What makes the most sense as the basis for the observed conduct? What are the personal meanings for the client? Try to set aside your own personal evaluation, which arises naturally from your own perspective, to become open to experience from another point of view.

Taking the Other Point of View

"If" can be a helpful word to evoke your sensitivity to possibilities. Ask yourself, "If I were in that circumstance what would I think and feel?" Try to imagine yourself in the other person's field of meaning, with the other person's background. In most cases a reaction takes place. You may get in touch with meanings similar to those of the client.

Write out a description of a typical problem in therapy you are familiar with, a common problem you might deal with. First, express it as experienced from the therapists point of view. Be explicit, without using jargon or diagnostic terminology. How does the client look and talk? How are the relationships affected? Now describe and express the problem from the client's point of view. How does the world seem to be? What would the client feel and say about the problem? Try to vividly imagine the experience, as quite real. Compare. You can apply both perspectives for therapy, in order to understand and help. Now can you invent strategies to assist from the perspective of personal understanding?

Inferring other people's perceptual fields can be a great exercise for enlarging your own field of meaning. The skills you gain from this are useful in many applications, including your personal relationships. When we understand we can usually relate better. But genuine relating is therapeutic, so do not over analyze for meaning. Sometimes a tactful honest personal reaction can be very helpful.

TIMELESS TEACHINGS

INFERENCE: LEARNING TO USE YOUR OWN FEELINGS AS A GUIDE

You can learn to infer the client's underlying attitudes, beliefs, and experiences from what is expressed. The expression is not just in the words. Your own feelings can become a guide to what the client is feeling. Learn to use your intuition as a guide. This exercise is designed to train in this important skill.

Pay attention to your own experiencing as you listen to your client. What do you feel as you listen? What meanings are being expressed? Focus on vague feelings that may be evoked in you. Then attempt to describe to yourself, in non-evaluative terms, what the meaning seems to be. Sometimes you will have an image or thought come to mind that seems incongruous or unrelated. You may discover an intuitive understanding of the problem, which goes beyond the obvious and rational. Sometimes, if appropriate, these images can be tentatively shared with the client. If you have been empathically linked, your image may stimulate understanding. It may make sense to the client, and if so, there is an inner confirming sense of its fit. But if not, let it go. Your client may not be ready yet, or perhaps you have not inferred correctly. Intuitive inference is not infallible. Try to not impose your inferences.

Do not rush inference. Apparent intuition may or may not be related to true perception of the client. Sometimes, you may discover yourself so much in touch that you know more than the client is ready to talk about. But other times, you may be misguided, due to unaware personal reactions to the meanings, including resistance and identification with the client. Mature therapists know themselves, and learn to be able to tell the difference by their inner signals. Mature therapists are also willing to grow. Do not avoid therapy or supervision if you deem it useful for you or your client. But often, the reactions you have to your client's therapy are enough to work on, to learn from and grow. Be sincere.

Empathy can be cultivated and imaginatively enlarged on, so that your inferences keep pace with the client's evolving process of understanding. The therapist is committed to help the client. Therefore, your client must be the center, not you.

REFLECTING FEELINGS

Reflection of feelings is one way therapists can offer their observations of the client's meanings. The client can clarify his or her self-concept in reaction.

The following technique is useful for reflecting feelings, but please use it sparingly. In keeping with the sincerity and genuineness that Rogers so wished for in therapy, beware of superficially imitating the technique; use the technique as an open pattern.

> *Express in your own words your understanding of essential attitudes and meaningful feelings of the client in the session. The factual content is not the essence. Disclose what you experienced to your client and ask for confirmation, whether you are on track and empathizing accurately. Accept feedback gracefully.*

Novice therapists sometimes just repeat the same words the client has used. The point of reflection is for the therapist to express the underlying feelings, not simply the specific content. An implied benefit of the reflection technique is to indirectly encourage the client to trust the expression of feelings. And the client's feelings are the focus. Then personal meaning can become clear for the client.

REFLECTING OBSERVATIONS

Another form of reflection is to reflect what is observed in the client's behavior, especially if it seems to imply meaning. This can be especially useful when the client's nonverbal behavior seems inconsistent, contradicting his or her words. But remember Combs' caution that there is no benefit to be gained from confrontation. It can lead to threat, which may interfere with the process. Permit your client to explore the personal meaning and discover significant patterns. Try not to interpose your own. This requires sincere modesty and self-discipline.

> *Observe the posture, gesture, tone of voice, and eyes of the client. Do not just reflect back the obvious feelings. Try describing vague background behavior that seems inconsistent. For example, "You say that you feel happy about that, but your voice sounds tight, loud, and you are leaning forward in your chair. What does this mean? I am unclear." Don't communicate in a confrontational manner, but rather in a way that provides nonthreatening feedback to enhance inclusion in the field of conscious self-awareness.*

REFLECTING MEANINGS

> *Reflection moves from the area of the explicit, what the patient is aware of, to the implicit, areas that are less conscious or unconscious. By using skill in empathy, you can sense possibilities*

of meaning in your client's statements. Then you can work together to clarify your client's feelings. Do not impose your personal interpretations or rush ahead. Client response should guide the process, so let the client guide you.

A meaning can be described in words, and imaginatively compared to the original nonverbal feeling for fit. Then if necessary, another word or words can be chosen to express the meaning. After expressing the meaning clearly, the vague background feeling is returned to for confirmation. Interaction between your reflections and your client's responses helps to clarify your client's feelings. But do not direct the client's experience.

For example, a man in a therapy group was making vaguely negative statements about his father. The therapist said, "It sounds as though you feel angry at your father." The man replied, "I don't think so. Not exactly."

"Are you dissatisfied with him?"

"Well, yes, in a way".

"Maybe you're disappointed in him?"

Quickly the man responded, "That's it! I am disappointed that he's not a strong person. I think I've always been disappointed in him, ever since I was a boy."

The therapist in this example gave space for the client to get in touch with the deeper, true feeling and discover its personal meaning so that he could come to terms with his father.

As you work with the perceptual field approach to the client you will find your own sensitivities develop. Theodore Reik, the noted psychoanalyst, stated many years ago that the therapist listens with the third ear. In time you will be able to intuitively hear the inner cadence expressed by your clients and use that to guide them toward personal growth.

Part Four

Milton H. Erickson M.D.

Photo taken in Dr. Erickson's
backyard following a seminar.

*And I think it should be interesting to you
consciously to discover many things that
your unconscious mind already knows and
is willing to share with you.*

Milton H. Erickson

Chapter Ten

Enlisting the Unconscious for Change

Milton Erickson was the founder of indirect hypnotherapy. He developed a method of treatment that was uniquely his own, utilizing his background, personality, and resources. During his lifetime, Erickson was considered one of the foremost hypnotists in the world. He benevolently influenced all who knew him. He helped to bring hypnosis acceptance as a powerful tool for psychotherapy. Today, the Milton H. Erickson Foundation in Phoenix, Arizona and Erickson Institutes around the world continue to use, teach, and propagate his effective approach.

Erickson creatively overcame a number of disabilities: He was tone deaf, color blind, dyslexic, and became completely paralyzed from polio at age seventeen. Through an intense two-years of self-discovery, he applied the hypnotic ideomotor effect (where an imagined idea becomes translated into an action response in the body) to find his way back into normal movement.

Erickson attended the University of Wisconsin for his MA and MD. He held a number of hospital positions, eventually serving as Chief Psychiatrist at Worcester State Hospital in Massachusetts. He published his first paper, showing what his research had demonstrated, that hypnosis was not a feared dark art but a safe and helpful tool. He performed much of his research during his years as Director of Psychiatric Research (1934-1939) and Director of Psychiatric Research and Training (1939-1948) at Wayne County General Hospital located in Eloise, Michigan. He then accepted a position as Clinical Director at Arizona State Hospital which he held for one year. But Erickson's health once again presented a challenge, when he suffered a second extremely rare attack of polio at fifty-one. This prompted him to open a private practice office at his home in Phoenix, close to his supportive wife, Elizabeth.

Erickson's disability in no way stopped his creative work. He taught widely as a guest lecturer, collaborated with many great minds such as Aldous Huxley to study effects of hypnosis. He researched and developed time distortion with Dr. Linn Cooper, helped found the American Society of Clinical Hypnosis, and served as its first President. He wrote numerous papers which were gathered together into four volumes by one of his most devoted students, Ernest Rossi. Erickson's fame spread, bringing students from around the world to learn from the master in his modest home-office. All who studied with him experienced firsthand his unusual perspective on psychotherapy and hypnosis.

Erickson's strategic interventions always evolved from his deeply felt empathy for human suffering. Based on how he had helped himself overcome his own disabilities, Erickson's approach masterfully combined hypnosis with active therapy to mobilize the unconscious for creative learning, problem solving, and change.

Our first appointment to see the famed hypnotherapist, Dr. Milton Erickson was set for eleven am, Monday, in the summer of 1977. Little did we suspect as we set out for Phoenix from San Diego that our scheduled one hour appointment would become an intense three-day experience!

Our single previous encounter with the desert had been at night, when we drove across the country from the East Coast to begin our graduate program in California early in spring. We amusedly remembered that the only rain we encountered on the entire trip was in the desert. We had formed a concept from this first experience that was, unknown to us, unique to that time of year. We were ill prepared for the dry, raging inferno as we descended the eastern side of the San Diego mountains. We did not realize that our concepts of what was possible and comfortable were soon to be changed. Only the wise know what they do not know.

We battled the suffocating 110-degree heat, construction, and traffic to arrive precisely at eleven am. Dr. Erickson's office was off to the side of his modest ranch-style home. We were ushered welcomingly by Mrs. Erickson to a back office building, peaceful and charming. The anteroom was about ten feet by ten feet, well lit from a window facing the grassy lawn, which set the area back from the road. A large photo of the famed French hypnotist Charcot hung on the wall over the door to Erickson's private office. The walls were paneled. Some simple chairs and a small couch were arranged in a circle, with one wooden-armed easy chair. The room was unpretentious and cozy. We passed the sitting room where five or six students chatted quietly, then entered Dr. Erickson's small office. This area was filled with many varieties of memorabilia, a cluttered desk, several chairs, a file cabinet and a bookcase. Hypnosis classics were in abundance. We noted a purple telephone that matched Dr. Erickson's purple leisure suit and shoes. He looked up, smiled at us with a twinkle in his eye, and invited us to sit down. He had a dignified, yet relaxed way of sitting in his chair, gently holding his hands together. He had fine features and a kindly warmth that filled the room with his benevolent presence. He asked, "Well, tell me, why have you come to see me?" Then he leaned back and watched us, one eyebrow slightly raised, as he waited.

We thought a moment, then replied, "We are graduate students in a doctoral program. We learned to do hypnosis with G. Wilson Shaffer who is at Johns Hopkins University back in Baltimore. We read about you through Jay Haley's books [the only writings on Erickson at that time] and found your approach fascinating."

Erickson smiled very slightly, as he paused, seeming to study his recollections. "I know of Dr. Shaffer, but have not met him personally."

We continued, "Our goal is to learn to enhance our capacities as hypnotherapists and to learn more about your method."

We told him about our work at our university counseling center, where we performed hypnotherapy. Our services were very popular, so we carried a caseload of up to ten clients each week, both students and staff. We described several clients and asked for his ideas.

Our discussion was not limited to hypnosis and hypnotherapy. We told him that we both enjoyed the practice of magic and misdirection. He said that he loved magic and asked us to show him some. Alex performed an old favorite, a heads and tails guessing game, where the coin is placed under a cup. On the third try, the cup is removed revealing not the expected coin, but a red rubber ball. Erickson laughed in enjoyment of the illusion. Then he turned it into a teaching situation.

"Direction of attention is one of the fundamentals in hypnosis. I like to direct attention inward, to an object of imagination rather than to the outer surroundings. This sets the patient on the path to trance."

We asked him the question we asked all our teachers, whether he believed the nature of man is good or not. He responded, "I believe there is something of value in people that needs to be expressed. Through hypnosis people can learn to do that." He asked us about ourselves, our training, graduate school experience, and goals.

Next, he called in a girl who had come to see him for therapy. He put us on the spot, so to speak when he said, "Annellen, please hypnotize Mary." He observed carefully while Annellen induced trance using suggestions for relaxation, comfort, and inward focus. After a few minutes Dr. Erickson indicated that he wished the client to be awakened.

"How do you feel," he asked Mary, "after having been hypnotized by Annellen?"

"Very relaxed and comfortable!" He looked at her, significantly. As she recounted her experience of being hypnotized she blinked and began to slip back into trance. Erickson encouraged her to reenter hypnosis.

"Now, close your eyes and let your trance develop naturally. Your arms and legs are relaxed, reflexes slowing." Then he said to us, "You can see that with her recollection of trance she began to slip back in. I merely directed her ever so gently, and her unconscious did the rest."

We watched him intently and noticed that he observed Mary closely and very sensitively. He seemed to be relaxing himself. His voice was calm and had a soft tone. He sensed our gaze upon him and turned to us to direct our understanding of what to do.

"Watch the client, not me. All the answers are there with the client, not with me." He continued to speak softly to her, deepening her trance until her head slumped forward and her entire body appeared limp.

At this point, Dr. Erickson motioned to us to leave so that he could concentrate privately on therapeutic work with her in trance. We got up quietly and left the room to join the other students, introducing ourselves. We hoped that we had done well.

Erickson was in great demand, as we were only just beginning to realize. One might wait almost a year for an appointment to study with him, to be integrated into a time frame in his busy appointment schedule. Only medical professionals, psychologists, social workers, or full-time students in graduate programs were permitted to attend his seminars. People came from all over the world seeking the renowned Milton Erickson. Some brought difficult cases for his critique or advice. Others requested his assistance for minor therapeutic growth. Through his seminars and private tutoring, Erickson taught and inspired his students.

Time passed and the door opened. Erickson gestured with his hand for all of us to enter his tiny office as Mary left. We all squeezed in awkwardly. The air conditioner hummed loudly during the session, but did maintain a bearable temperature. He spoke softly, and the hum made his voice indistinct to the group.

He said, "If the air conditioner bothers you, I can turn it off. I can have it either way: I use hypnosis to feel as cool as I want to be." We asked him to turn it off so we could hear better. With the air conditioner off, the summer Phoenix sun baked the little office to a sweltering temperature. We all began sweating, but true to his word, Erickson remained cool and comfortable. He had gained an amazing ability to control his body.

He asked us, "Do you know the difference between a buffalo and a bison?" When we all looked at him blankly, he mocked surprise and said, "What, you mean to say you don't know the difference? Well, every Australian knows that a 'bison' is what you wash your 'fice' in!" We all laughed and applauded after we realized he was using a homonym. He had begun to extend our consciousness of meaning and culture.

One of the students asked, "How do you work with patients who have multiple problems?"

Erickson answered, "The patient gives you a long story. You listen to it and try to recognize the main problem. Once you have it, all the rest tends to fall into place. A six year old boy didn't know what was what. He was retarded, and I could see that this hurt his parents, not the boy. They felt that he did everything the wrong way. He felt badly about his parents and did everything he could to make them feel better. I said to him, 'If you can't get your shoes on, you can't get to the breakfast table.' This got him motivated to get his shoes on properly. I added another problem to the multiple problems. When you correct one thing, you're correcting, by implication, a lot of things. They get straightened out in a hurry when you make it tough for them."

Next, he passed around the writing of a patient and asked us all if we could determine what the patient's problem was. Every other word was reversed. There were many speculations among the group but Erickson denied all our hypotheses. Finally he explained. "As soon as I saw Eddie's writing, I invited him to exercise his imagination and knowledge by reading the chapters of a book backwards. I told him how Hemingway, under certain psychological circumstances, took more than a page to wander into a story and to wander out. I was delighted to explain to Eddie that his character wandered into the story under certain circumstances as well. I told him that he was an American citizen, old enough to be his own person like any good citizen. Now, I could have labeled him, but every case and person must be individually evaluated. I've seen many patients, from Gestalt, psychoanalysis, and other psychotherapies who have been instructed to conform. Every individual is his own person. Once Eddie started thinking for himself his writing improved. When you truly understand the patient's problem, you can help him. But don't assume that the patient knows what his problem really is," he said with a twinkle in his eye. "Clear, thoughtful analysis to determine the true problem comes first."

Erickson's country lifestyle background, similar to other great practitioners like John C. Whitehorn, gave Erickson a down-to-earth, confident, and at-ease quality that was deceptively disarming when coupled with his wisdom and knowledge of the world. Without seeming to be, he could be brilliantly subtle in therapy with ordinary everyday people, as well as with the sophisticated professionals who studied with him. Erickson could communicate however he needed to.

Although best known for his extraordinary work with hypnosis and trance, it would be a mistake to assume that Erickson always worked in a trance, or that his hypnotic work has no relevance for psychotherapy apart from an hypnotic orientation. He drew from the wisdom of his unconscious functioning, but he was also a very rational and conscious professional psychotherapist. He believed in facilitating each individual. He said, "All children develop in their own way. Too many doctors and lawyers expect their children to follow them. This destroys the child 's future if there is no interest. When doing psychotherapy we help patients to find their own interest: who they are and what they are.

"I once treated a lawyer with his son. The lawyer wanted his son to take over the practice. But the son made a mess of it. I said to the son, you are not interested in keeping up dad's business, so go get yourself a job, a menial job. Pay your own bills and live on your own earnings (even though his wife was independently wealthy). So he worked as a gas station attendant. He ate hot dogs while the rest of the family ate steaks. After two years, the lawyer's son went back to take over his dad's business, and he did a much better job having chosen it himself. Some people have to find themselves. When people are maladjusted, it can be very helpful to shift their line of work for a reasonable length of time."

Erickson sometimes did the unexpected. He had a way of bewildering his students so that they were open to learn. He would send people out of sessions and bring others in, adding an air of mystery and surprise to the experience. At a certain point in the midafternoon of the first day, he asked us to go to a restaurant nearby where they served excellent Mexican food, while he rested. He promised to return later in the afternoon to continue the seminar.

At the restaurant the participants spoke about their experiences with Erickson's indirect suggestions and teachings. Each was certain that there had been a story meant for him or her. Students maintained that Erickson had intended specific themes only for them. Everyone felt amazed by his subtle sensitivity. It was clear to us that he had a way of presenting the material so that every listener felt deeply involved in a personally meaningful way.

When we returned to his office, Erickson recounted many stories of a wide range of patients with all types of problems. He spoke of the wonderful enjoyments of farm life and drew strength and comfort for himself and his patients from the natural sources of American folklore. Erickson was concerned that individual patients and students did whatever they did well and with enjoyment. If married, Erickson tried to get them to treat each other better. He helped people work well while having fun in other areas of life as well. The same logic applied across the spectrum of humanity.

Erickson's unique approaches derived from his own efforts to overcome such difficulties in his life as dyslexia, color blindness, and tone deafness. He told us, "I consider these advantages because they taught me not to take things for granted. I'm not distracted by tone and color. I can discern shades and pauses in voice that others usually miss." He learned to use all his experiences in positive ways.

Erickson believed that the hypnotherapist needs to be flexible and open-minded; rigid sets or frames of reference could become limitations and obstacles to treatment. "I had been working with a patient for many months and I felt like we were getting nowhere. So right before his next session, I went into a trance and used amnesia to forget I had ever known him! Then when the patient walked into my office, I met him as if for the first time. I had a fresh perspective which made the difference."

Erickson often spontaneously went into trance during therapy. Trance meant a focused, concentrated state of awareness. When he was teaching, his empathy and imaginative involvement were so intense that while describing a hallucination for his patient to experience, he empathized with great intensity, almost seeming to participate in perceiving it too.

People at the seminars often went in and out of trance. Once at a seminar we attended, Erickson asked a student, "What did I just talk about?"

The student answered, "I can't remember, I must have fallen asleep."

Erickson responded, "Now think for a moment. Your unconscious mind remembers exactly what I was talking about and knows that you have done some learning."

The student thought for a moment. Her eyelids closed slightly and her body relaxed. Then she opened her eyes wide and smiled. "Yes, you're right! I remember exactly what you said." And she recounted the story, adding in the meaningful associations she had for herself. Erickson guided her into applying her unconscious intelligence.

Erickson was acutely aware of subtle distinctions most people never notice. He used everything he was aware of to help the treatment process, including wisdom from his unconscious. Erickson drew from his vast knowledge from observing mechanisms of mind along with commonsense practical understandings of human nature and incorporated them into techniques of suggestion. "An eight year old girl hated everyone. She spent all her time hating. I asked her mother, 'Why is she so unhappy?'

"Her mother answered, 'Freckles'. There were multiple ways of expressing her ire about her face. But she chose to stay shut up in her room. I went into her room to see her and I said, 'Where did you get that Cinnamon face?'

"Years later I got a call from a woman. She said she wanted a favor, not therapy, but to come in to get a frank opinion of her appearance. I said, come on in. I looked at her carefully and said, 'The ring on your finger indicates you are a married woman. Your hair is well combed, eyebrows have nice curves, your eyes are very beautiful, and your cheekbones fit your face, which is very well shaped. Your lips are full but not too full, nice chin and a good complexion.' In fact, she was very well-formed and appeared to be twenty-six or seven.

"She said to me, 'My name is Cinnamon Face.' I had not seen her since she was eight years old. She returned to Phoenix to proudly show me how she looked now. But when she was eight years old she had hidden her face. Just this year I got a Valentine from Cinnamon Face."

We were to return many times over the next years, finding that each time was different. As Erickson's work became interpreted by theories such as Rossi, Bandler and Grinder and Haley, people came to learn from him, through the lens of these views. Erickson skillfully crafted stories to help them learn, yet also made it clear to us that his method was always multifaceted.

He cared about his students and facilitated their individual lives and needs. He often encouraged his students to learn by trying hypnosis on themselves. At one seminar, Annellen was due to give birth to our second child within the month. She expressed an interest in using hypnosis to ease her labor pains during the birth of our son. We felt that, as practitioners of hypnosis, it made sense to experience the process for ourselves.

At a certain point during this seminar, Erickson instructed Annellen to gaze at a chunk of natural quartz crystals on his desk. He suggested that she become progressively less aware of externals and focus her attention inwardly. Then he asked her to close her eyes and enter trance deeply. He encouraged hand levitation and general anesthesia. "You can be fascinated with naming the baby up until the very moment of birth. You might wonder what the little fingers and little toes will look like." She found herself comfortable and grateful for his efforts. In the actual situation of childbirth, we did use hand levitation and anesthesia during the contractions to successfully deliver with a normal pulse rate and respiration without drugs.

Over the years, he took a special interest in our young children. He invited our daughter and son, in turn, to sit with him, and allowed them to attend the seminars with us. He always looked for ways to help. Our whole family looked forward to visits with Erickson whenever we could.

His stories contained many lessons for his students. "The wife of a rancher developed generalized arthritis and became very depressed. She was treated with surgery that was unsuccessful. She wanted very much to have a baby, but her arthritis got worse and worse. She became suicidally depressed. The rancher took her to many psychiatrists, but he did not want her in the hospital. He wanted to take care of her himself. He carried her in and out. She said that life without a baby wasn't worth living. I told her that if she got pregnant her arthritis could improve. She could have a caesarian. She did become pregnant and had the baby, but it died a crib death after six months. The wife became suicidally depressed. The rancher brought her back to me and I told her, 'You ought to be ashamed of yourself. You had nine happy months carrying Cynthia. Now you are going to commit suicide and throw away those months. And you had six months with the baby, and you will destroy those memories!' I directed her to plant something and name it Cynthia. I told her that she should be ashamed to destroy fifteen months of good memories. Years later, I saw her. Her arthritis improved and she was still growing Cynthia. I often give patients something to take care of. When they see a plant begin to grow, or an animal develop, their attention has shifted, and they feel better about themselves." This was one of his many techniques, created when necessary.

The courage to explore and develop new ways of psychotherapeutic intervention is rare. Erickson was a pioneer in bringing a sensible, socially responsible, yet individualized treatment into the arena of hypnotherapy. His focus was on meeting the needs of the patient, and he was critical of therapists who turned away from patients who sincerely sought help but were ambivalent, resistant, or difficult to treat. His discoveries in these areas, expressed in his papers and seminars, were groundbreaking and courageous. One of his special interests was "impossible" cases: he enjoyed meeting the challenge of helping them resolve their difficulties and he had a lot of fun doing it.

The people in life who benevolently and idealistically help us grow and develop are few. Learning from Erickson was an unforgettable experience that set positive forces in motion for us. We are grateful for our time with him and will continue to integrate the learnings. Erickson dedicated himself unselfishly to hypnotherapy to benefit others. We know that his creative brilliance will always continue to inspire and guide future generations of therapists, as he would have wanted.

Chapter Eleven

Creative Approaches to Therapy

And in any psychotherapeutic situation, whatever the school of thought which predominates, there must be recognized over and above the formalized structure of thinking, the importance of the patients themselves. (Erickson 1980 Vol. I. 541-542)

EXPERIMENTAL METHOD

Erickson's views of hypnosis and psychotherapy were based on continual research he conducted throughout his lifetime. He thought deeply about what his experiments revealed and applied the results in his practice. He continued to learn and grow.

Erickson's experimental curiosity started during his childhood on the farm. He first began to understand resistant behavior, one of his specialties, from an experiment he conducted on the family calf. His father was unable to pull the stubborn animal into the stable. Young Erickson discovered a solution. He pulled hard on the tail while he directed his father to continue pulling on the collar. The calf chose the less adverse of two stimuli and went into the stable dragging Erickson with him. Erickson traced his comprehension of the principles of resistant technique to that experience.

Erickson's early formal training in hypnotic research began as an undergraduate student at the University of Wisconsin. He attended a seminar on hypnosis given by Clark Hull from 1923-4. Erickson began formulating some of his ideas through this interaction with Hull. He learned about the manipulation of attention and observed ideomotor phenomena, both of which became important in Erickson's approach.

Hull was convinced that the hypnotist controls the subject's experience. He also believed that hypnosis is merely a heightened form of suggestion. Erickson felt in strong disagreement and conducted some experiments to test his ideas. He worked with a subject to develop hypnotic phenomena, which he demonstrated for Hull and the seminar. Then he began to research the nature of hypnosis.

Subjects were told that the experiment was devised to learn more about the introspectionist theory of thinking. Subjects would follow their thought about a task from start to finish. He asked subjects to imagine a bowl of fruit on a table and visualize moving each piece of fruit from one place to another. Half of the sixty-three subjects could not perform the task and stopped midway. The other half who were able to imagine the task exhibited similar reactions that resembled hypnotic phenomena. Their breathing slowed, they lost the blink reflex, their eyes closed, and their dominant hand exhibited ideomotor phenomena, i.e. the hand raised and lowered, seemingly by itself. This early research and later studies with hundreds of subjects showed Erickson that:

> The less the operator does and the more he confidently and expectantly allows the subject to do, the easier and more effectively will the hypnotic state and hypnotic phenomena be elicited in accord with the subject's own capabilities, and uncolored by efforts to please the operator. (Erickson 1964, 154-57)

Erickson found that hypnotic techniques worked best when tailored to fit the needs of individual personalities and the needs of the person's specific situation.

Research on hypnosis should take this individuality into account but seldom does. Erickson believed that hypnotic research could be unobtrusive and naturalistic. He attempted to correct the problems of using the experimental method to study hypnosis by his development of naturalistic approaches to supplement his formal empirical studies. He engaged in extensive research throughout his life, using both methods to explore as well as develop his effective approach to hypnosis and psychotherapy.

Some of his experiments were informal mini-experiments, performed wherever he was. He discovered his confusion technique from a spontaneous experiment he performed. One windy day on his way to the seminar with Hull, a man came rushing around the corner and accidentally bumped hard against him. Erickson took this opportunity to perform a naturalistic experiment. He looked down at his watch and acted as if the man had asked for the time. He said very politely, "It's exactly ten minutes of two," even though the actual time was closer to four, and quickly walked on. Half a block away Erickson turned back and saw the man standing absolutely still on the corner watching Erickson with a puzzled expression on his face. (Erickson 1964, 183-207) This gave Erickson insight into confusion, which he learned to use for therapy.

Erickson believed that clinical trance is different from experimental trance. He considered much hypnotic research poorly conducted because it did not take this distinction into account. One important difference was that hypnotic researchers did not take adequate time to induce a good trance. In his experiments, Erickson took the time needed to produce a deep trance in each of his subjects. He trained them carefully in hypnotic skills, as he would with a patient in therapy. Much of Erickson's extensive research was done as in-depth work with each subject. He sometimes spent as much as twenty hours to produce a profound hypnotic trance before beginning the research. As a result of this careful induction work, his subjects were able to develop profound trances during experiments, producing many variations of hypnotic phenomena. Erickson drew conclusions from his experiments that helped him develop his method of hypnotherapy.

Rather than seeking a comprehensive theory of hypnosis as a total phenomenon, Erickson researched individual manifestations of hypnotic phenomena and related them together. He believed a comprehensive theory was premature. Standardized induction methods are antithetical to the nature of hypnosis and give a false image of what takes place within the individual. Researchers can best come to understand the phenomena by careful observation and notation of what he called, "the unique, varying, and fascinating kind of behavior that we can recognize as a state of awareness that can be directed and utilized in accord with inherent but unknown laws." (Erickson & Rossi 1980 Vol. IV, 349)

Erickson devoted his career to observing and recording hypnotic behavior. He continually experimented with suggestion and trance over the years. He applied hypnosis with great success to problems within the personality as well as problems in relationships. He was careful, as a committed doctor, to use his research findings to enhance the quality of his therapy. He made many discoveries to help deepen our understanding of modern hypnosis and effective therapy.

STRATEGIC, ACTIVE PROBLEM-SOLVING

A proper therapeutic goal is one that aids patients to function as adequately and as constructively as possible, to use their tendencies in positive ways and yet meet their needs. (Erickson & Rossi 1980, 397 Vol. IV)

Erickson's theory was deeply integrated with his working techniques. For him, clinical techniques served a purpose. Erickson's focus was the patient's actions. His work was multifaceted, defying categorization. His techniques mobilized people to act differently as well as to think and feel differently.

Erickson viewed the life cycle as a continuum, with certain skills expected and challenges to be met at each phase. He looked for what was preventing his patients from flowing with the natural cycles of their lives. Then he applied his knowledge of human nature in creative ways to help patients solve problems, resolve conflicts, and move forward. His active form of treatment helped get people back on track.

In the midst of an insight-oriented psychoanalytical climate, Erickson boldly focused instead on what troubled the patient. He was willing to meet the needs of the patient rather than impose lengthy analytical treatments that had only vague application to specific life-problems. As time passed, his approach evolved into an individualized treatment for the patient. He broadened the scope if necessary.

Action therapists put special emphasis on results. Action therapists do not expect insight to bring change. Insight is used sparingly, only if it facilitates change. Conscious understandings of motives and patterns matter mainly in terms of the resolution of the problem. Erickson was part of this tradition, though not limited to it. He believed that insight often obstructs change. There are times when patients do not understand how they change. In fact, sometimes Erickson himself did not always try to understand why a patient improved; this was not important to him or the patient. As he once said, explanations are like attempting to summarize a Shakespeare play in one sentence. The primary goal of therapy was clear: bring about beneficial change.

One of Erickson's formulations for therapy was to decide what the patient's main problem was. He stated in his seminars that therapists should define the problem in their own way, not according to Jung, Freud, or even Erickson! Once the main problem is solved, he explained, all the others will fall into place. The therapist's thoughtful involvement matters.

People learn through action. When they have new experiences, they begin to make changes. In order to help bring about change, Erickson often prescribed tasks—an action that the patient agreed to perform. In one case, (Zeig, 1980) a couple, both psychologists, had been in therapy for ten years. They continued to have marital problems as well as professional difficulties. Before Erickson would set up a session with them, he required that the husband climb Squaw Peak [a nearby mountain park in Phoenix] and the wife go to the local botanical gardens. Upon their return, the wife reported that she felt bored doing the task. She was angry about having to waste her time. The husband had a very different experience. He thoroughly enjoyed the climb and thanked Erickson for the experience. Next, Erickson instructed them to switch tasks. Once again the husband found the task stimulating while the wife felt her frustration mount. The third task was that they choose for themselves. The husband returned to the botanical gardens and the wife returned to Squaw Peak, with similar results as the previous day. After the couple returned home, the wife immediately filed for divorce. She said that she realized when she performed the tasks how stuck she felt in her life. In contrast, her husband was inspired by his experience and began to reorganize his own therapeutic practice, an endeavor he had been neglecting for years.

Erickson's prescription of treatment was not standardized or limited by time. For example, he did not see clients only on a weekly or twice weekly basis. Nor did he always structure sessions as a fifty-minute hour. He was flexible, adapting to each patient's situation as he perceived it. The needs of the patient are the primary concern.

PART FOUR

LEARNING CONTEXTS

Among the many and varied patient-therapist interchanges, Erickson often determined if his patient needed to learn something. In a seminar the authors attended, Erickson stated that many patients in therapy have deficits in their early learnings, due to their preoccupation with problems. (Seminar in Phoenix, April 1979) The WAIS information section shows that psychological disturbance can lead to gaps in common knowledge. Erickson's therapy helped people undergo the learning they needed to overcome such deficits. He used automated functioning that was already part of the patient's repertoire to help facilitate appropriate learning.

Erickson found many possible ways to utilize everyday functioning to create a context for learning. For Erickson's patients, therapeutic learning could take place anywhere—even when going out to dinner, climbing a mountain, or visiting a museum.

The general context of a situation can be used for the therapeutic purpose of affecting behavior. For example, Erickson once created a situation for a young male patient who suffered from an inability to cross certain streets and enter certain buildings without fainting. The patient was shy and fearful, especially around attractive women. Erickson invited the patient to attend dinner at a restaurant with an attractive divorcee and Dr. and Mrs. Erickson. With the help of the waitress and the female dinner guest, Erickson proceeded to put the patient through an intensely uncomfortable, embarrassing but manageable therapeutic experience. Afterwards, the patient felt that having survived such discomfort, he could handle anything. Following that evening, he gave up his fears. (Haley, 1973) Erickson would probably have agreed with Gestalt Therapy founder Fritz Perls' construct of learning in therapy: Learning is the discovery that something is possible. (Perls, 1969) With Erickson's ingenuity, any situation could become a therapeutic learning context to help his patients change. With Erickson's help his patients learned to make the impossible possible.

MENTAL MECHANISMS OF MIND

Erickson also used mechanisms of learning to help people change. Mental mechanisms are already present, derived in part from earlier understandings and experiences and in part from common human nature. They function outside of conscious awareness. Erickson thought it essential to use what was already there in patients to help them reorganize and relink their potentials. He considered the individual's innate learning mechanisms to be one of the many devices built into the mind that could be adapted for therapy.

THE MENTAL MECHANISM OF ASSOCIATION

The concept of association in mental functioning is as old as psychology. Aristotle described it in his theory of the mind. Traditionally, it has been stated that associations, and the capacity to form associations, are the most characteristic aspect of the human mind. (James, 1896) Therefore an idea can be communicated by association. Associations are stimulated naturally during therapy. Erickson used this mental mechanism creatively to communicate ideas in his therapy. Associations may be evoked by attributing meaning to objects, gestures, and other events and experiences in therapy. The essence is in the meaning's function and communicated intention, not in the object itself. Various classes of response reaction may be evoked using association.

Once the response has been evoked, the therapist may ask for a response, enlarge on the response, and thus gradually gain the capacity in general to influence and thereby help the patient change. When Erickson felt that association would be helpful for his patient, he might use an indirect suggestion about association, such as "The foot bone is connected to the ankle bone..." to help direct attention to make an associative link.

Guthrie, a learning theorist in the classical tradition, believed that learning *is* association. He believed that people learn because they make the association, not because they expect a reward, though a reward may come. Reinforcement or reward is irrelevant, and learning may take only one trial. (Koch, 1959) Simpler, general understandings become the foundation for compound, more complex ways of functioning. But sometimes people unintentionally learn things that are not beneficial.

Erickson advised therapists to respect and comprehend patients in terms of their own personal meanings for associations. He often helped his patients return to the sources of the problem, to help reorganize and reinterpret experiential learning in new ways. Then his patients formed new patterns drawn from their own inner resources.

Directing patients' attention to their own capabilities can bring about useful therapeutic learning experiences to help them. Similarly, Erickson helped patients discover an unrecognized resource and then guided them to apply this resource in association to current problem areas. In one of the seminars we attended Erickson described the case of a man who felt desperate because he could not write. Erickson asked him if he knew how to hold a pencil in his hand. He said he did, and demonstrated. Could he draw a straight line and a circle? The man said of course he could do that. Erickson then carefully guided him in combining and reorganizing these learnings. He showed the man how the entire alphabet could be reconstructed from learnings the patient already had, but did not think of using to solve that problem. This analogy can be applied broadly.

Sometimes people need to reinterpret similar abilities from other unrelated areas of functioning and apply them creatively. For example, people may not know how to do automatic writing, a phenomena produced in trance. But most people have doodled unconsciously while talking on the telephone, or tapped their fingers to a song without intending to. Sometimes people flinch while watching a boxer on TV get a hit, or duck down when something is thrown at someone in a movie. These types of unconscious reactions can be generalized from and used for automatic motor responses. Such responses help tap into undeveloped potentials for automatic writing in hypnosis.

Erickson also used association by pairing an unpleasant experience with the symptom. Behaviors that are troublesome can often be made less inviting if people associate them with something they dislike or wish to avoid. But Erickson did not assume that behavior is simply determined by negative or positive reinforcement: The success of this technique requires a therapeutic rapport as well.

Erickson's work illustrated the use of this mechanism. An insomniac was told to polish his hardwood floors whenever he could not sleep. An overweight woman was required to walk to the store each day and buy only enough food for that day. By pairing the troublesome habit with an unpleasant task, these patients were able to give up their symptom. This was only one of many creative applications.

Erickson devised a set of suggestions he called the "early learning set" using skills acquired early in life to build new ones. For example, a toddler first learning to walk illustrates the virtue of trial and error random efforts, from which eventually the child discovers how to walk. The errors are eventually dropped or forgotten. The correct responses remain, so that the person can walk efficiently. Mistakes are part of human learning; we learn from our mistakes as well as our successes. This can be a useful lead-in for encouraging the patient to try other ways. The confidence gained from successful accomplishments of difficult but simpler early learnings is also a basis for trust that later complex learnings can also be possible.

THE NATURAL TENDENCY FOR LEARNING TO GENERALIZE

Another mechanism of mind is the natural tendency for a partial response to generalize or lead to a total response. Erickson used this mechanism with numerous patients. A pattern of behavior that is any fraction of a larger response can elicit or extinguish the larger response. For example, we had a patient with intense general nervousness. She had been on Valium for some years, but still felt anxious. She learned to go into a deep, relaxed trance. We suggested that she could be less nervous in one manageable context, her dance class. Through her trance work she learned to experience all her nervousness in her little finger. While her little finger would shake, the rest of her body remained calm and steady. This and other similar experiences helped her discover her unrecognized ability to be calm when she needed to be. One day her purse was stolen along with her medication. She never refilled the prescription. Instead, she viewed this as an opportunity to use her newly found skills. She soon did not feel she needed medication and went on to become calmer in her daily life.

Sometimes the meaning context of learning has to be shifted in order that transfer can take place. The original meaning may limit its usefulness when applied in other contexts. Mental rigidity is a distinguishing feature of neurosis, according to Kubie. (1975) Flexibility in application of learned sets or expectancies is important for mental health.

As part of his teaching seminars Erickson sometimes brought in patients for students to actually observe him at work. One time when we were visiting, a patient came to Erickson to quit smoking. Erickson asserted that he would not treat her for smoking until she performed a certain task for him. Before accepting a patient, he usually asked if the prospective patient would comply with whatever he required, promising that the task would not be harmful. This patient agreed to do whatever Erickson asked. Erickson usually demanded this commitment whenever possible, to help in the inevitable resistance to therapy. Erickson said, "Your task is to climb Squaw Peak. When you get to the top look around carefully, and then report back to me." And, he added casually, "Oh by the way, leave your cigarettes here in the office with me." Several of the students asked to accompany the patient on the climb. On the way up, she grumbled and complained that this seemed to be a stupid waste of time. But once at the top, she took a deep breath of clean mountain air and enjoyed the majestic view. Upon her return, she went to Erickson and told him that she did not need him, hypnosis, or cigarettes. He just smiled, benevolently.

SYMBOLIC LEARNING

Learning situations give patients the opportunity to observe themselves and learn what they want and need by working on deeper issues symbolically. For example, once Erickson worked with a patient in her thirties. Her initial reason for treatment was to understand the spontaneous trances she had at home. But as the sessions progressed, she began to recognize troubling emotions from childhood that interfered with her present life. Erickson used symbolic language and fantasy to work through the traumatic material. (Erickson & Rossi 1979, 377) When she imagined herself swimming, going deep underwater and finding shells, Erickson interpreted that she was probing psychologically. By working with him on a symbolic level, she could unknowingly explore potentially painful experiences without pain. Through Erickson's careful guidance, she found a personally meaningful resolution for herself. Erickson used the personal metaphors of the patient. He was comfortable using anything that facilitated the therapeutic process. With this patient Erickson talked about shells and water to express the therapeutic process of change and growth. With other patients he used different metaphors that suited them.

The therapist does not always need to know exactly what the patient is referring to by the symbols or exactly how they may need to digest or assimilate the therapeutic material derived from it. Erickson once told us that it was a mystery how patients developed their problems and a mystery how they lost their problems. He respected the unknown and learned to use sophisticated unconscious therapeutic abilities.

EXPECTANCY

Erickson pointed out that just as an attitude of expectancy can influence the results of an experiment, the attitude taken toward our capabilities in ourselves will influence what becomes possible for us to do in hypnosis, in therapy, and in life. (Seminar in March 1978) Erickson encouraged therapists to allow patients to use their own capacities, including their expectations, hopes, and attitudes to assist them in therapy.

Erickson believed that the therapists' expectancies can also profoundly affect the results they get from their patients. In experiments he performed, Erickson found that the expectancies of the experimenters, communicated by minimal cues such as voice tones, deeply affected the performance of the subjects. Subject tended to exhibit the limitations of the operator's expectancy about what they were capable of. These experiments, performed long before Robert Rosenthal's well-known later studies on expectancy and experimenter bias in research were corroborated by Rosenthal's findings. (Rosenthal, 1969) Erickson carefully worked to expand his students' capabilities to free them from their own limitations so they would not limit their patients.

Erickson not only used expectancies to facilitate the therapeutic process, but he also upended expectancies in order to assist patients in reorienting to what was possible for them. Often therapeutic change requires that patients alter their view of themselves and their resources. Erickson was fond of presenting puzzling cases in his teaching seminars. Students found themselves thinking of new creative ways of construing patients and problems. A wide range of techniques can derive from the use of expectancies, hopes, and attitudes to respond.

Pseudo-orientation in time was one technique directly used by Erickson to capitalize on the positive use of expectations, hopes and wishes. Erickson invented this technique from his creative discovery that if a person could fantasize that they regress in time, they could also fantasize that they progress in time. This discovery could be applied to help patients develop favorable expectancies and methods for relief. People often came up with solutions by imagining having successfully achieved them. The boundary of time did not limit Erickson or his patients. And it should not limit other therapists or patients either.

This technique was formulated by a utilization of those common experiences and understandings, embraced in the general appreciation that practice leads to perfection, that action once initiated tends to continue, and that deeds are the offspring of hope and expectancy. (Erickson & Rossi 1980 Vol. IV, 397)

TIMELESS TEACHINGS

THERAPEUTIC RELATIONSHIP

The therapeutic relationship was vitally important in making Erickson's hypnotherapy effective. In fact, one of Erickson's first goals was to establish an intense relationship. The intensity of the relationship does not just happen, but is a product of the way the therapist deliberately relates to what matters to the patient and how the patient relates in response. Erickson cared, and his patients knew it.

Therapists should protect the needs and dignity of patients while undergoing therapy. Patients' needs and personality should be met whenever possible. For example, if patients feel a need to be private, they should be encouraged to keep a secret from the therapist. This helps to develop trust.

Erickson believed an intense therapeutic relationship might require the range of human feelings. Erickson's interactions could be challenging. Patients might feel rebellious, angry, guilty, and many other negative emotions. Erickson expanded the concept of the therapeutic relationship to include the negative from patients and even negative from him when he thought it would help. Erickson knew that such experiences could be beneficial. Including contrary, resistant feelings allowed patients to receive therapeutic ideas, and thus benefit. But skill and tolerance is needed by the therapist

Erickson cited many cases where patients would prove him wrong and thereby get over their problem. He described a boy who continued to wet his bed for years. Erickson told the boy, "You will not stop wetting the bed this month, but you might later." After a series of these types of time injunctions, the boy defied Erickson and stopped on his own time schedule, not Erickson's. (Seminar, 1979)

In many cases patients would become angry with Erickson and "curse him out" for demanding them to do something they thought to be "a stupid waste of time." As one patient told Erickson, "I hated you horribly, you made me so furious, and the madder I got, the more I tried." (Haley 1967, 540) This annoyance allowed patients to discharge some of their negativity so they then could begin to take positive steps toward change.

Students of Erickson were often mystified as to how Erickson could get his patients to perform some of the difficult or absurd tasks he asked them to do. Erickson explained that he always gave such instructions with absolute certainty that the patient would find it meaningful:

His attitude toward me is such that, "Well, if Erickson says so, it's worthwhile." He doesn't recognize that it is he who makes my suggestions worthwhile. But I tell my patients that, and I mean it. It's the fact that I mean it. If they don't do it, I am genuinely disappointed and they know I am. (Haley 1985, 118 Vol I)

PART FOUR

Despite the fact that Erickson apparently took command, he always recognized that the real power for change lay in the patient's abilities and the patient's willingness to use them, even if the willingness was at a level outside the patient's awareness. Absolute faith in the patient's abilities mobilized within a strong therapeutic relationship, became a powerful force in Erickson's therapy.

THERAPEUTIC TRANCE AND THE UNCONSCIOUS MIND

Erickson used hypnosis as the primary mode of therapy. He believed that hypnosis allows therapeutic work to proceed effectively and efficiently. He often said that the trance facilitates learning that would take a much longer time in conventional therapy. He also believed that altered states of consciousness were the key to creative learning. Erickson felt that all of the major breakthroughs in his own life came under hypnosis.

Erickson distinguished between trance induction and trance state. Although some therapeutic work can be done during induction, the main work in hypnotherapy takes place through the "therapeutic trance," as he called it with Rossi (Erickson, Rossi, Rossi, 1976). He also differentiated the therapeutic trance from the experimental trance discussed earlier.

For therapeutic trance to be most effective, time must be devoted to carefully inducing trance. During trance induction, therapists should keep in mind the patient's actual wishes and needs. Erickson presented a wealth of related ideas carefully calculated to hold patients' attention to their own sensations, emotions, thoughts, feelings, and memories. Once the trance is developed, people become more receptive to any general ideas the therapist offers. They are able to examine, evaluate, and discover for themselves the applicability of the therapist's suggestions to their problems.

The essence of induction methods is to direct and hold patients' attention on their own experiencing, not that of the therapist. This inner focus allows people to do the unconscious work of therapy on their thoughts, feelings, learning, and behavior. The induction of trance facilitates and activates thoughts and associations within the patient. Learning and resources already present from earlier experiences are the source for the evoked responses.

Erickson led subjects step-by-step into trance phenomena. He was sensitive to the nuances of the subject's relationship to the trance situation, so that he could utilize how the subject responded in a myriad of multifaceted ways, as part of induction. When patients presented themselves for trance but expressed doubt that they could be hypnotized, Erickson recognized the ambivalence as part of their response. He believed that the therapist should accept ambivalence rather than attempting to change it. The therapist should weave together a tapestry of suggestion that includes both, so as to properly address and recognize both sides of the patient's feelings. These tendencies can be cooperated with and used therapeutically, to help induce trance and then work within its framework.

TIMELESS TEACHINGS

TRANCE UTILIZATION

Hypnotherapists offer stimuli to the subject but they should never delude themselves into believing they are the source of learning. Erickson asserted strongly that patients reorganize and resynthesize learnings themselves through the use of their own resources.

> In the therapeutic use of hypnosis, one primarily meets the patient's needs in the terms he himself proposes and then one fixates the patient's attention, through adequate respect for and utilization of his method of presenting his problem, on his own inner processes of mental functioning. This is accomplished by casual but obviously sincere remarks, seemingly explanatory but intended solely to simulate a wealth of the patient's own patterns of psychological functioning so that he meets his problems by use of his learnings already acquired or that will develop as he continues his process. (Erickson 1964, 32)

The trance is a state of focused attention and active unconscious functioning. This unconscious functioning tends to be uniform and universal in its features even though each person is a unique individual. Erickson was interested in unconscious understanding, and related to the unconscious whenever possible. This gave him an uncanny ability to sense and activate the very thoughts of his patients and students. In every seminar we attended, most of the members of the group found that Erickson's stories were meant for them personally.

Erickson's trance work permitted patients' unconscious mind to be dissociated from their conscious, so that they could work on therapeutic matters without interference from conscious resistance. Through the therapeutic trance, the unconscious can be appealed to directly. He believed that unconscious understandings should not be reintegrated before the conscious mind is ready. Sometimes, he came to feel it was not ever necessary for people to consciously know what they had learned unconsciously. In keeping with life's mystery and wonder, changes in behavior, thoughts, and feeling take place of themselves.

SUGGESTION: THE THERAPEUTIC TOOL

Erickson conceived of suggestion as the capacity to respond to ideas. He believed this to be a normal capacity everyone possesses, and he utilized it to help elicit change. (Erickson, 1961) In hypnosis, people can be responsive to suggestion, especially when there is a strong rapport.

Research on suggestion in the 1920's and 30's indicated its importance for psychotherapy generally. Schmideberg (1939) pointed out that

110

suggestion operates in all interpretations and interventions, whether the therapist intends it or not. According to Young (1931), the therapist's intentions not to be suggestive are not significant. Since suggestion operates by unconscious mechanism, it works automatically anyway, outside of awareness. The mere presence and attitudes of the therapist tend to have a suggestive influence on the patient, whether the therapist intends it or not. The suggestive influence gets stronger, the longer in therapy. Since it cannot be avoided, therapists should use it for their patients' benefit.

As was discussed by Frank in Part One, professional displays such as diplomas on the wall and pictures of eminent psychologists raise expectations, suggesting expertise, competence, and the appropriate setting for therapy to take place. When a therapist confidently presents his therapeutic system, it is implicitly suggested that the patient will benefit. All forms of therapy include an element of suggestion as a prominent and influential non-specific factor in therapeutic effectiveness. Suggestion pervades therapy.

Suggestion works best when it is in harmony with some inner impulse, ideal, or sentiment. Symonds (1958, Vol. III) recognized that once a pattern is stimulated by suggestion, it tends to have the right of way in expression. The narrowing of attention that hypnosis tends to elicit can enhance the effectiveness of suggestion. The combination of hypnosis with suggestion offers an excellent likelihood of therapeutic response, especially when hypnotherapists utilize what the patient brings psychologically to the session.

Erickson recognized these aspects of suggestion and went further. He enhanced and magnified the effectiveness of his suggestions by adding the automatic mechanisms of mind.

LITERAL UNCONSCIOUS AND THE INTERSPERSAL TECHNIQUE

Erickson found in his research that the unconscious mind responds literally whereas the conscious mind responds to implication and more complexity. He asked subjects in a trance, "Are you willing to tell me your name?" They always responded "Yes", but offered nothing further. When he asked people who were not in a trance the same question, they invariably responded by telling him their name. In other words, when people are awake they respond to implication, but in trance they respond literally. He also found that patients often consciously resist literal direct suggestions about their problems. Defenses come into play; doubts, resistances, and the structure of the person's difficulties interfere with responsiveness. But in trance, literal suggestions are listened to and considered (Erickson, 1980).

Erickson devised his therapeutic technique to contain literal suggestions to which the unconscious mind would respond. He couched these within intricate, complex subtleties to redirect, depotentiate, and distract the conscious mind from resisting.

Erickson felt that his interspersal approach to indirect suggestion was one of his most important contributions to suggestion. (Erickson & Rossi, 1979) This device was the backbone of his hypnotherapy. He created many elaborate and creative forms of suggestion that could be confusing shocking, vague, general, common knowledge, esoteric, fascinating, or even boring. All these intricacies distracted the conscious mind from the literal suggestions he interspersed for the unconscious. Through the combination Erickson was able to bring about therapeutic responsiveness even in difficult cases.

Interspersed suggestions operate on many levels by inserting a word or phrase here and there throughout a therapeutic session. These suggestions stimulate thoughts, images, and reactions in a certain direction. For example, a tense patient who cannot relax if asked directly to lay back and let go of tensions, will be able to relax when words implying comfort and calm are interspersed in a casual conversation couched in the language and subject matter typical for that patient.

Erickson not only interspersed suggestions into the context of conversation, but he also combined trance suggestions with therapeutic suggestion.

> ...During a technique of suggestions, for trance induction and trance maintenance, hypnotherapeutic suggestions can be interspersed for a specific goal. In the author's experience, such an interspersing of therapeutic suggestions among the suggestions for trance maintenance may often render the therapeutic suggestions much more effective. (Erickson 1966, 198)

This explains in part why Erickson chose to use hypnosis as the primary vehicle for therapy. He believed that the patient's unconscious mind is more responsive, less defensive, and a great deal more intelligent than the conscious mind. He trusted his patient's unconscious for therapy.

INDIRECT SUGGESTION

In keeping with his general approach to solve problems by stimulating the patient's own inner resources, Erickson developed a special form of suggestion: the indirect method.

The more traditional direct form of suggestion tends to use specific statements. These statements rely upon the motivations and voluntary cooperation of the patient to do what is asked. However, many people who come for therapy have found that their motivations and personality do not allow them to voluntarily resolve their difficulties. Erickson's indirect forms of suggestion help the patient become capable of accepting therapeutic suggestions necessary for change. Indirect suggestions explore and facilitate what the patient's response system can do on an autonomous level without really making a conscious effort to direct it. (Erickson & Rossi, 1979) Indirect suggestion uses the subtlety and complexity of patient responsiveness, especially around the problem areas. The patient's motivations and personality, along with the natural mechanisms of mind, are used in formulating indirect suggestions.

The best discoveries in therapy are those that occur to the patient spontaneously. Indirect suggestions offer hints of certain possibilities without filling in the details. They are deliberately constructed to encourage discoveries. We all have hypotheses about what learnings will be most helpful for our patients; but ultimately, changes must take place within the individual. Erickson would tell patients, "Healing takes place in your own way and your own time." And he believed it. This open-ended suggestion implies that the patient will make progress. The therapist indirectly suggests healing, but how this is to be is done is left to the patient.

A cut heals naturally of itself so long as the wound is cleaned and covered. Similarly, mental difficulties can be healed if circumstances are arranged so that constructive mental processes can take place of themselves. Therapeutic trance allows natural healing capacities to occur.

Erickson believed that therapeutic change takes place when people undergo an alteration of their internal world of experience: a change in the meanings, as Combs referred to it, or the assumptive world, according to Frank. This change involves reorganization and resynthesis of abilities people already possess. Erickson did not consider that he added something to the repertoire of his patients but rather helped them make better use of what they already had. Then transformation of meaning becomes possible.

The therapist should take into account the individual's personality, cultural milieu, and presenting problem in order to make suggestions to facilitate therapy. For example, talk about football will elicit the image of a different game for an American than a European. European "football" is the name for American "soccer." These differences should be addressed. Erickson took all of these factors into account in carefully preparing indirect suggestions for distracting the conscious resistance and eliciting personally meaningful learnings in his patients.

USE OF MINIMAL CUES

Indirect suggestion can be communicated through the use of symbols. A gesture, a voice tone, a glance, an omission, can all suggest symbolic learning through an idea or the class of ideas the therapist wishes to communicate. Memories can be linked to a place. We have all had the experience of listening to an old song and remembering where we were when we originally heard it. Sometimes smelling an odor reminiscent of an old storage attic will bring to mind the experience of being there years ago. Any sense experience can be used to elicit responses.

Erickson used both verbal and nonverbal minimal cues to communicate suggestions. Part of the apparent mysteriousness of his work derives from this subtle use of communication. He experimented with many communication devices, such as breathing rhythms, glances with a significant emphasis, pauses, and dangling phrases. His subtle use of voice, tone, and meanings evoked responses from the unconscious. His communications frequently defied attempts to discern them or identify how the response was brought about. His concern was change, not recognition.

OVERCOMING RESISTANCE

Indirect suggestions are not only used to improve responsiveness. Erickson devised ways to use indirect suggestions as a therapeutic tool to discharge resistance. Some of his most brilliant successes involved turning around a negative, hostile, uncooperative patient.

Erickson did not turn down patients due to unattractive qualities in them. He believed it was the duty of psychotherapists to help all patients who sought their help, no matter what they were like. His indirect suggestions took into account that patients have hostilities, guilts, stubbornness, and every variety of negative emotion and habit. In fact, these negativities can be useful material for indirect suggestions. Erickson was not afraid to utilize this negativity. He found that when he permitted patients to have the freedom to be negative, if that was how they felt, surprising and unexpected therapeutic procedures suggested themselves. He enjoyed the challenge of strategic intervention. Sometimes he shocked, surprised or confused his patients. He used these strategies to bring about a strong response in the context of his caring relationship.

Erickson characterized his resistant technique as based in meeting the needs and attitudes of the patient with acceptance, cooperation, receptiveness, and attentiveness. By accepting even the most negative reactions he could "quickly transform these overt seemingly uncooperative forms of behavior into good rapport, a feeling of being understood, and an attitude of hopeful expectancy of successfully achieving the goals being sought" (Erickson 1964, 8).

Transforming resistance into rapport is essential for all therapy, not just hypnosis. The fixed attitudes patients bring to therapy are easily evoked as a means of securing their concentrated attention. The resistant, negative patient often compulsively adheres to these attitudes. It can be fairly straightforward to encourage involvement and cooperation by accepting the patient's resistance to help them change.

Erickson believed that the clinician should utilize everything the patient brings to the therapy situation. Whatever participation the subject gives to the situation can be used. While he was conducting demonstrations of hypnotic phenomena, for example, he successfully hypnotized everyone who volunteered as subjects, even people who seemed to feel negative about hypnosis. When patients presented ambivalence about their problem, he used both the positive and negative motivations to help them change.

With patients who suffered from guilt feelings, for example, his manner while giving suggestions might be reprimanding or imply punishment at first. For example, Erickson treated an anorexic girl by scolding and punishing her. After she was cured she told him that in the midst of her illness she felt herself to be a very bad person. Now that she felt differently, she could recognize that she would not have believed Erickson if his suggestions had been positive and supportive. Because he had been negative, she took what he said seriously. (Erickson 1980, Vol. IV) Then he could guide her toward health.

Erickson addressed the complexity of the human mind by using complex, multilevel, compound suggestions. Compound suggestions often include opposites of the same idea in one suggestion. The "apposition of opposites" (Erickson & Rossi, 1979) works with the common dynamic that patients are often in conflict between opposite tendencies such as tension and relaxation, remembering and forgetting, love and hate. The apposition of opposites uses negativity in a positive way. He reorganized patients' inhibitory or oppositional tendency, by phrasing suggestions to include opposites or negatives. These suggestions guide patients to begin altering the inner fabric of their difficulties. Compound suggestions can be created from simpler ones, as the therapist's skills evolve.

CONCLUSIONS

Erickson's legacy continues to break down rigid perspectives and inspire new and creative approaches. The aspects of Erickson's work we have described here can be used by psychotherapists of many varying approaches to compliment their methods. Even if only in reaction, the reader may discover new ideas, concepts, and creative applications. Perhaps this personal, individual response is what Erickson would have wanted from his students, after all.

Timeless Teachings

Chapter Twelve

Utilizing Suggestion and Trance

The patient comes to you with a long story. Find their main problem. The rest falls into place. Good judgment in this is needed, not a formula for a criterion of clinical acumen. (Erickson, Seminar in Phoenix, January 1980)

The therapist should not assume the client's presenting problem is the fundamental problem. Focus on the most important component of the individual's problem, which might not be obvious. For example, we had a client who came in for treatment for a fear of flying. However, after careful questioning, we learned that the patient's husband was an amateur pilot who loved to fly. She was very angry with her husband. Her real problem was her relationship with her husband. When this was resolved, she no longer feared flying.

The reader may wonder how to develop his or her clinical acumen. Erickson's answer to this question was to point to the client. The client is the source of therapeutic change, not the therapist. Be observant. What is the client saying and doing during the session? And what does the client bring to the session as a deeper concern? How would you describe this client to a colleague? Is there any significance evident to you in what the client is exhibiting? Consider such clues from language or clothing as possible metaphors rather than just literal meanings. And most importantly, your client should be the focus, not your own ideas, concerns, or theories.

Use your reasoning abilities to deduce what the main problem is and how to work with it. Let your chain of reasoning lead you back to the real problem, your starting point for hypnotic therapy. Erickson believed in meeting the client's needs. Inference can lead you there.

Sometimes the problem will emerge in clearer form through the course of treatment. The wise practitioner keeps an open mind as new information uncovers new possibilities. When the true difficulty is understood, what suggestions should be presented become clear.

MAKE ONE SMALL CHANGE

Erickson sometimes would begin a change process when he asked his patient to make one small change. He believed that making a change in one area will often generalize. The authors used this with a patient who wanted to lose weight and feel less stressed in her everyday life. She was told to make one small change. She decided to have her hair permed. This started a chain reaction. She said later that the ten minutes she saved in the morning by not having to curl and style her hair made her whole day less hectic. She arrived earlier at work, had time to orient to the day, and felt in a better frame of mind. As a result she worked more efficiently and well. Everyone at work appreciated her change in attitude. This small change opened the possibility for her to make the larger, necessary therapeutic change resulting in a calmer lifestyle and the successful loss of weight.

HYPNOSIS: THE USE OF SUGGESTION AND TRANCE

As explained previously, suggestion is inherently part of all therapy, whether the therapist deliberately uses it or not. You may use suggestion with or without trance. When used without trance, suggestion can help enhance and facilitate therapeutic learnings. When used with trance, suggestions can be even more helpful, since in trance people often feel receptive and open. If you find that you would like to go further with self hypnosis, we recommend our book *Effective Self Hypnosis, Pathways to the Unconscious*, written for both laymen and professionals who would like to integrate self hypnosis into their work and their lives. Training in clinical hypnotherapy can be gained through programs offered by the Milton H. Erickson Foundation seminars and affiliated Ericksonian institutes.

SUGGESTION

Understanding suggestion requires recognition of the subtleties of conscious and unconscious process. We have all experienced suggestion spontaneously in many forms. For example, when you are expecting someone to call, extraneous sounds suggest the telephone ringing. Many people have experienced induced suggestion after watching a horror movie or reading a frightening story. Shadows may take on a scary appearance when normally they go unnoticed. These are examples of spontaneous suggestion. This ability of the mind to make suggestive links can be used deliberaterly. Then suggestion can work for you.

One way to understand the deliberate use of suggestion is to experience it for yourself. Experiment with the ideas and exercises presented to personally experience suggestion. The following is an exercise drawing upon one fundamental of suggestion: A vividly imagined idea tends to have a corresponding response in the body.

Close your eyes and think about a tart lemon. Imagine this as vividly as possible. It you have salivated, you have experienced the effects of suggestion.

Suggestion operates when it is in harmony with some inner impulse, sentiment, or ideal. Erickson devised his suggestions to draw upon mechanisms of mind, experiences, or ideas common to all people or specifically relevant to the individual patient. Your client's response will indicate whether the suggestions are useful. Suggestions you think will be helpful may not be meaningful to your client. For example, if you are trying to help an anxious client feel more relaxed, draw on that person's natural abilities. Look for hobbies and interests for resources, times when the client has naturally experienced relaxation, and build upon these.

YES SET: READYING FOR SUGGESTION

The use of suggestion requires planning and thought to be most effective. Erickson spent many long hours alone in his office carefully constructing exact suggestions that would be most beneficial for each of his patients.

From the moment the client enters the office, you can begin encouraging therapeutic change. You can create a climate that will help the client feel comfortable and open to therapeutic suggestions. Erickson called this a "yes set" or "acceptance set". He often began a session by being agreeable himself and talking about things of likely acceptance that most people would agree with. On a sunny day, he might say, "Today is a beautiful day." You can compose truisms to cover many subjects. A truism is a simple statement of fact we have all experienced so frequently that we cannot deny it. This helps encourage agreement, facilitating beneficial influence.

Another way to create a yes set is when you talk to clients about something they find interesting. For example, you might begin by saying something about sports to an athletic man. By arousing his interest you can draw his attention to the conversation.

But honest interest matters, not false interest.

You can also get people's attention by showing them interesting objects. For example, the authors have a number of abstract paintings by the artist who did the painting on the cover of this book. When asked, people always have a definite idea about what the painting represents, yet each person's view is different, activating personal interest and inner search. Erickson often used humor as well. He had an object mounted on the wall that he called Count Dracula. Objects of personal interest tend to focus attention and make people feel comfortable in the office. Objects that arouse curiosity along with the yes set help to bring clients into an agreeable, open state of mind, making them more likely to accept the benefits of treatment. This supplements the more formal display of diplomas and pictures of teachers that Frank believed can raise expectancy of help.

USING DIRECT AND INDIRECT SUGGESTION

Direct suggestion occurs when you tell people exactly what they are to experience and they experience it. Rossi stated it succinctly, "Direct suggestion...presents subjects with a stimulus that identifies what the results should be." (Erickson, Rossi, & Rossi 1976, 268) An example of a direct suggestion is: Become more relaxed. You are feeling more relaxed and calm.

Indirect suggestions are usually more effective for psychotherapy than direct suggestion. The purpose of indirect suggestion is to make the idea you present inspire clients in their therapeutic process. Most therapists have used indirect suggestion whenever they tell a client about another person, in hopes that something will be learned. This method of suggestion will often bypass resistance that might arise from a direct suggestion.

Recognizing the suggestive aspects of your own therapeutic approach can be helpful. Examine your work in terms of its suggestive qualities. Here are some commonly used indirect suggestions that tend to mobilize clients toward positive responses to treatment. But sincere belief in your system has this effect automatically. These kinds of statements tend to come to mind spontaneously during therapy:

--This therapy has been helpful to other people with problems similar to yours. Perhaps it can help you too.

--If you try this (referring to a therapeutic technique you want the client to do—e.g. charting or listing in cognitive-

behavioral methods, sensing emotions in humanistic therapies or other appropriate technique) you will have an interesting experience (or new understanding, insights, or awareness.)

--After this session and all the work you did today, you may begin to feel some change.

These are just a few common examples, but you will undoubtedly discover your own suggestions you may not have noticed before embedded within the method of therapy you perform.

Suggestions have many benefits besides the direct idea or action you intend to communicate. People feel reassurance when they are doing what is healthy and positive. When people respond to suggestion, they often feel like the suggestion occurs by itself in a natural way. This encourages confidence in the treatment, raises self-esteem, and lowers anxiety.

The essence of therapeutic suggestion must be sincerity. Without your sincere intent as a professional for the welfare of your client, suggestion is ineffective. Search for the sincere intent of your therapeutic method and then be true to it. This gets communicated to the client and has a positive suggestive effect. Your honesty and true wish to help will benefit your client, as well.

THERAPEUTIC TRANCE SERIES

Hypnosis is first and foremost an experience. Learning to use hypnotic trance with clients is best begun by experiencing it for yourself. The following exercises show you how to go in and out of trance. Before you begin, find a comfortable place where you can sit or lie down and some free time when you will be undisturbed. You can begin with as little as five minutes, but you will probably increase the time. Trance is a skill like any other and responds to practice. Do not be discouraged if you do not seem to feel anything at first. Eventually you will be able to recognize the subtle indicators and enlarge on them to enhance your experience.

READYING FOR TRANCE

Sit or lie down and relax for a few moments. As you relax, let your thoughts drift and your attention roam wherever it likes. Try not to get lost in any one thought-path; simply notice associations and let them go. Do this until you notice some settling or calming.

EXPERIENCING TRANCE

Sit quietly and allow your thoughts to drift. Let your body relax and breathing become comfortable. Let go of any unnecessary tensions. When you feel relatively relaxed, turn your attention to your hands. Notice whether your hands feel a sensation: warm, cool, tingly. Ask yourself whether one hand feels heavier, warmer, cooler than the other. Wait for your spontaneous, unconscious response.

Allow the experience in your hands to develop. Let your arms become heavier, warmer, cooler, etc. As this happens, suggest to yourself that, if your unconscious is willing, you could become even more relaxed. Can you recall a time in your life when you have been very relaxed, without trying? It may perhaps have been when reading a book, enjoying the company of friends or family, or walking in nature. Permit your spontaneous response and memories to emerge. Then concentrate on your experience, as deeply as you can. Continue to breathe comfortably and relax even more, letting the feeling spread. Permit yourself to enjoy your own natural resource. Regular practice will enhance this.

AWAKENING FROM TRANCE

When you feel ready, you can awaken from trance. One common method is to count backwards from five to one. With each number, suggest that your sensations gradually return to normal until you reach one, and you feel refreshed and alert. Moving in and out of trance becomes easier with practice. Repeat the trance series over several days and weeks to deepen your trance experience. Your personal experiences will enhance your client's experience; as you learn to accept your own unconscious, you will learn to accept your client's unconscious, the source of positive potential.

Part Five

G. Wilson Shaffer Ph.D.

Photo taken in Dr. Shaffer's office
at The Johns Hopkins University

While each method possesses certain unique and distinctive characteristics, they are not mutually exclusive. Within the framework of each distinctive therapy, certain features of other methods are utilized.

G. Wilson Shaffer

Chapter Thirteen

Working Harmoniously

G. Wilson Shaffer was a pioneer in the field of clinical psychology. His tireless work as writer, practitioner, teacher, and administrator contributed to the widespread practice of clinical psychology today. He co-wrote two early volumes which became handbooks for practice all over the world. His first book with Roy Dorcus, *Textbook of Abnormal Psychology* (1945), is a classic in the field of abnormal psychology. It went through four editions and was translated into many languages, including Braille. He also wrote a handbook for students, *Fundamental Concepts in Clinical Psychology* (1952) which clearly presented the path that clinical psychology has developed and evolved in modern times. His other area of expertise was hypnosis. He used hypnosis to treat students at his clinic for decades. His professional papers explained varied topics such as hypnotherapy, the nature of intelligence, and the therapeutic value of recreational sports. He also wrote a well-regarded study of the history of recreational sports at Johns Hopkins.

Shaffer joined the staff of the Sheppard & Enoch Pratt Hospital as Psychologist in Chief in 1928 and continued there into the 1970's At the same time he was also Chairman of the Department of Psychology at Johns Hopkins University and Director of the Athletic Department. Later he became Dean of the University and at times, when needed, dean of a number of departments simultaneously. A tireless worker, Dean Shaffer founded the Psychological Clinic at Johns Hopkins University in 1935 and continued to direct until his retirement in the 1970's. He was the first Diplomate in Clinical Psychology in the State of Maryland. He also founded the Maryland Psychological Association and served three times as president.

Shaffer's scope of understanding spanned psychiatry, psychology, sociology, and counseling. He sought communication and cooperation among helping professions for the good of the client. Unlike some psychotherapists, Shaffer refused to limit his approach to one methodology. He chose instead to integrate and use apparently opposing systems of therapy, adapting them sensitively to the individual client's needs. He orchestrated differing approaches together smoothly and naturally, to find their common ground. True to his beliefs, he looked for synthesis and found it!

Shaffer was well known in Baltimore. He had earned a reputation among college students for being able to help rapidly, turning the tides of students' lives to flow in the direction of the positive, even in impossible situations. Shaffer was always available to help whenever anyone at the University had a problem. Robert H. Scott, Lacrosse Coach and Athletic Director for some forty years, stated, "Dr. Shaffer had a superb way in dealing with people. His wisdom was surpassed only by his compassion, sensitivity, and gentleness. Our coaches gave Dr. Shaffer, with affection, the nickname of 'The Swami'. Whenever one of our athletes would get in trouble or have a problem, we would say, 'Send him to The Swami. He will give him a few Z's and take care of him.' Sure enough, he would." His skill with positive suggestive influence was legendary.

Dean G. Wilson Shaffer was such a charming, warm, and friendly person that we felt comfortable with him from the first moment. We were very interested in learning hypnosis as part of our training and he agreed to supervise us in these learnings. He was retired at the time of our studies with him, but had retained an office at Johns Hopkins University.

Shaffer's office was located on the Johns Hopkins University campus in Homewood House, a white wooden building in the traditional cottage design. The secretary, who greeted us as we arrived, gestured to some worn narrow steps leading down to his office in the basement. We found our way through several corridors and downstairs to a large room, mostly empty except for a desk at one end with several chairs in front of it and some bookcases to the side. At the far end, Shaffer rose from his desk and bid us to come in. He pulled out a side chair to pair with the ones already facing his desk. Smiling, we sat down and gathered ourselves for the appointment.

Shaffer looked up at us with an affable, engaging expression. His eyes were clear and candid; his ears had long lobes, with a lot of character. His smile was broad and welcoming. Though in his seventies, he was vibrant and energetic, with a large chest and wide shoulders. An atmosphere pervaded the room of calm, rational goodwill and well-being. We quickly felt at ease due to his charming manner.

We explained, "We are students, committed to learning to be the best psychotherapists we can be. We have heard of your renown with hypnosis and therapy and hoped to learn to use hypnosis as part of our therapeutic technique."

He smiled and responded, "I will be glad to assist and supervise you. I do have some experience. Our clinic here on campus has been active since 1935, although I have just recently retired." He modestly neglected to tell us that he had founded the clinic and had been its director for forty years. Osmar Steinwald, the former Director of Alumni Relations at Johns Hopkins University called his clinic, "Revolutionary. There weren't many places a boy could turn to then. Many are still grateful for his guidance."

PART FIVE

Schaffer had a sense of humor and joked about his office location. As he put it, "When you've been around as long as I have, they keep you on, even if it is in the basement." He firmly believed that if you were a good person and a hard worker who does his or her part, the institution would work with you, not against you. Shaffer Hall at Johns Hopkins University was named in his honor, symbolizing his continuing presence. His many leading positions with numerous institutions held over such a long period of time are testaments to the efficacy of his philosophy!

"How do we start to induce hypnosis?" We asked.

He leaned back in his chair thoughtfully. Then he smiled as a warm look appeared on his face. "Please stand up Alex," he asked. "Now close your eyes. As you are standing there, you will feel yourself falling backwards." He stood behind with his hands ready to catch Alex. Alex instinctively trusted Shaffer and felt confident that he was benevolently helping us to learn. So Alex allowed himself to have an interesting experience. Later we were to learn that a trusting relationship with the hypnotist is an important variable in the effectiveness of the suggestions. Alex felt himself sway backwards slightly. Dr. Shaffer said, "This is the postural sway test for suggestibility."

Next he turned to Annellen. "Interlock your fingers in front of you and clench your hands very tightly together. You will find that your hands become locked together and you are unable to unclasp them." The feeling of her hands being locked together was an odd one. Dr. Shaffer masterfully introduced us to the phenomena of suggestion and their application in such a natural manner that we were able to learn without concern for resistance or threat, a hallmark of his teaching approach. He showed us a number of classic and modern suggestion techniques. He explained that these could be used to measure suggestibility and to start a person moving toward trance for therapy.

Step by step he showed a simple method of inducing trance. We walked through suggestions to relax and go into hypnosis. He encouraged us to add small, subtle touches of artistry to help make the hypnotic experience more vivid for the client. He gave as an example, "Perhaps you are talking about galloping horses." Then he started to drum his fingers on the desk, a sound to match his words as stimulus for the subject to weave into the experience. "Other creative variations are possible," he said. He encouraged us to try hypnosis with our clients and assured us that the judicious practice of it need not be harmful at all with proper supervision and precautions. He watched over us carefully, guiding our progress in understanding. After a number of teaching sessions, he saw we had learned enough to begin to help others.

Our first hypnotherapy client was a woman in her early twenties, recently divorced who had returned to her home state of Maryland with her four-year-old daughter. She felt uncertain of what direction to take in her life. She hoped to reestablish a relationship with her father who lived in Baltimore, but felt incapable of doing so. She was intrigued by the mystic arts, and found hypnotic suggestion appealed to her as a treatment modality. She wished to lose weight and felt hopeful that the hypnosis would be helpful in all of these areas. Shaffer skillfully guided us in discovering her therapeutic needs and helping her evolve.

Shaffer had an uncanny way of knowing a great deal about the client even though he might have only third-hand data. As W. G. Fastile said of Shaffer, "He did not need to talk very much. It was uncanny, but he could look you in the eye and know exactly what you were thinking." We experienced this over and over again in our work with him.

He listened carefully to our first taped interview and said, "I wonder if she would find it meaningful to be a social worker?" Later we told her what he had observed and she responded with surprise that she had nearly gone into a social work program the previous year. He also asked us the age of her ex-husband. He correctly predicted that he was older. She described herself as "spacey" and complained that she often felt rushed and hurried. He noted that there was a significant relation between her eating disorder and her use of time. This later proved to be one of the central issues in her problem.

Shaffer guided us in suggestive therapeutic methods. Our client was from an ethnic subculture. He pointed to lines of inquiry, to comprehend her personal, interpersonal, and cultural dynamics, and then to work with them. He showed us a strategic, active intervention, interweaving suggestion into therapy.

"Has she had many disappointments?" He asked.

"Yes, quite a few in her life," we answered.

"Suggest to her that she has suffered enough. Give her suggestions that she can control herself; and that she might find something else to give her comfort. Emphasize that, instead of her eating." Under his guidance, we used suggestion to present alternatives to our client, to reduce her symptoms and improve her functioning, helping her substitute more fulfilling behavior. She improved steadily. At the end of treatment she decided to enter graduate school to pursue an advanced degree. Her father welcomed her and they were able to work out a positive relationship.

Shaffer helped us to let go of our stereotypes and fixed beliefs about what was typical or possible. Discussions were expressed on a common-sense level. His comments sometimes seemed simple on the surface, but he had a way of getting to the heart of the problem. A young lawyer had a problem with his temper, which was becoming a detriment for him professionally. He asked us to help him gain control.

Shaffer said, "Use suggestion to calm him down, to suggest that he could control his feelings of anger and not need to express them irrationally."

We asked him, "If we make these kinds of suggestions, isn't it possible that worse symptoms might be activated?"

Shaffer responded, "Many times clients simply calm down. Experiment, and we will work together to help moderate and then improve his response"

This was exactly what happened. At the next session we induced trance. Our client chose to look at three amusing ceramic monkeys sitting on a shelf, "See No Evil, Hear No Evil, and Speak No Evil" as he went into trance. Once he was deeply hypnotized, we suggested hand levitation. We observed that his hands twitched slightly and sweat beaded up on his forehead, but he exhibited no signs of actual hand levitation. When he awoke, he disclosed that he felt very embarrassed because he had probably made a fool of himself doing jumping jacks with his arms flailing up and down, right in front of us. From this imagery he learned, by analogy, that he need not express in overt actions all of what he experienced or imagined inwardly: indeed, his inner experience could be vivid and much more intense than showed outwardly. This was a reassuring insight for him. Over time his impulsive behavior due to temper outbursts diminished and then ceased altogether; and he felt calm enough to work out difficulties more rationally. He developed excellent self control. As an evolving professional, this mature attitude was beneficial for his career.

Shaffer was amused and intrigued when we played the session tape for him. When we described the details of the hand levitation technique we had used he said, "Oh yes, I first did that one about fifty years ago." We were always amazed at his breadth of experience over time. We asked him whether we should insist on conscious awareness of his personal psychodynamics, to ensure that our client would not develop some other symptom due to the presumed pressure of an underlying conflict. Shaffer smiled reassuringly as he explained that desensitization and reeducation through suggestion often does not need analytic insight for change. He explained that in his experience insight was not always needed. Milton Erickson incorporated this in his work, as well.

We also discussed another area we all felt to be pertinent to mental health— athletics. Shaffer valued recreational sports highly. He believed that in play important lessons are learned, which can be therapeutic and valuable to the psychobiological functioning of the whole person. Under Shaffer, intramural sports at Johns Hopkins were expanded and the entrance fee to all college sports events was abolished. The free admissions policy was revolutionary at the time, lasting for thirty years. He explained to us, "This allowed anyone to just drop in to watch a game. People need recreation, either through playing or the enjoyment of watching a good game. It is fundamental for a healthy adjustment." Years later, the Ivy League schools followed his lead: he was a man ahead of his time.

At one of our meetings we discussed marriage therapy. He told us, "Recently I was asked to give a lecture to a group on marriage. But I told them, 'Why don't you find someone with more experience, like one of these guys who has been married two, three, four times. I've been happily married to the same woman for fifty years. What do I know about marriage?'"

He also liked to answer people who asked him why he had no children, "I have about five thousand sons!" (At that time Johns Hopkins University was an all-male school.)

We always looked forward to our appointments with Dr. Shaffer.
We stopped seeing him when it was time for us to leave Baltimore for further graduate study: our doctoral program in San Diego. The comprehensive learnings we had gained from him became an important part of our professional practice.

Chapter 14

Integrating Methods

Grasp the whole of Reason, Life, and Sense,
In one close system of Benevolence;
Happy as kinder, in whate're degree,
And height of Bliss but height of Charity
God loves from whole to parts: but human soul
Must rise from Individual to the Whole.

(Alexander Pope)

G. Wilson Shaffer's work helped shape psychotherapy as it is practiced today. In order to understand the links it is helpful to put him into his historical context. When Shaffer was practicing psychology in the 1930's and 40's, treatment of the mentally ill lagged far behind treatment of physical problems. The medical sciences of the time were unsophisticated about the psychological realm. Methods of psychotherapy continued to be slowed by efforts to distinguish between psychological and physiological functions. Psychologists played a lesser role in treatment.

Shaffer was one of the early voices to speak out for the importance of psychologists in treating mental illness. "Mental illness must proceed from the recognition of the individual as a psychobiologically integrated organism" (Dorcus 1956, 449). Shaffer explained that the individual functions on three levels simultaneously: The anatomical, involving the relation of the organs to each other, the physiological, containing the biological and neurological, and the psychological, encompassing the relation of individuals to their environment. Disturbances at any level can affect the integrated activity of the person, and therefore they all need to be treated. Knowledge and expertise of psychologists could integrate with the therapeutic treatment of the whole person in mental hospitals. Shaffer demonstrated in his own career that this was not only possible, but also extremely favorable.

The situation began to change with the greatly increased demand for treatment as a result of World War II. The psychiatric field was understaffed and turned to psychologists for help. (Shaffer & Lazarus, 1952)

Shaffer's first text was designed to address the need for psychological training for psychiatrists. He was audacious and visionary in condemning misuse of electroshock and certain chemical interventions as assaults masked as treatment. He proposed using psychotherapy instead and clearly stated the methods for his readers.

To truly understand the client's difficulties, the cooperation of many disciplines working together is best. He believed that a partnership was desirable and positive. Medical sciences, sociology, anthropology, along with psychology could team up to really learn the most about clients. In his own work, he was always a team player. Perhaps this was exemplified in the many roles he played. He integrated knowledge of many disciplines to learn as much as he could about all aspects of the client's current life, environment, and history. Then he took this information into account to help in the synthesis of his clients.

PREPARATION OF THE PSYCHOTHERAPIST

Shaffer recognized that there seem to be many opinions about how a psychotherapist should be trained, but they share some common factors. Primary was that psychotherapists should fully know themselves. Many of the problems clients bring for treatment touch upon our common humanity. Therapists who have thought deeply about these issues and dealt with them personally are better able to help others. Good therapists have searched deeply within.

Often problems have an environmental component. The therapist should understand social conditions and how they affect people. This understanding should extend not only to knowledge of different cultures, but also to different social stresses that can have real effects on psychological functioning. Shaffer believed this understanding would permit thorough, individualized treatment.

ASSUMPTIONS FOR PSYCHOTHERAPY

As Shaffer observed, certain broad assumptions are shared by most psychotherapists. A fundamental assumption is that behavior is lawful, not random or meaningless. This becomes the basis for the psychotherapist's work. Similar to how Sherlock Holmes followed the inner thread of his cases, the therapist learns to reason from behavior to grasp inner psychological dynamics which follow a lawful path.

Another important assumption is that people are motivated. Many behaviors arise from biological drives and social motives. People do not usually know what really motivates them; therefore clinicians cannot trust the simple self report. They learn how to infer motivations indirectly, usually from behavior or what the client says in therapy.

PART FIVE

The motives of an individual tend to be consistent, acting like a system for that person. Some call this system the personality, others the assumptive world, the belief system or self concept. The psychotherapist tries to identify the client's consistent style of thinking and reacting along with the typical modes of defense, for optimum clinical intervention.

Processes totally or mostly outside of awareness lead to behavior patterns.. These processes are what Shaffer referred to as the individual's psychodynamics, through which people interact with and are in turn acted upon by the environment. When Shaffer talked about psychodynamics, he did not mean repressed instincts, ego, or id of psychoanalysis. He blended together the best from aspects of the classical personality theories. Shaffer's personal approach to psychotherapy focused on the whole person with his or her unique personality as it was expressed in daily living. He took into account both the client's individual perceptual field and external factors when he assessed client's problems.

How Problems Develop

People become disturbed when healthy functioning is blocked by learned patterns. These patterns develop over time into symptoms and emotional disturbance. The psychotherapist attempts to decide where the disturbance originates and forms a treatment procedure accordingly. To best understand the client's disturbance, Shaffer asked himself the following questions: Why is the client having a problem at this time? Why did the disturbance take the particular form exhibited? What accounts for the manifested symptoms?

Shaffer first took a detailed history of the circumstances surrounding the earliest memories of the problem. The constitution of clients and their habitual patterns will give clues about the form of their disturbance. Collaboration with other team members with expertise in those areas is often helpful. Medical practitioners could, for example, determine the physical factors that are involved.

The family's perspective may be quite different from the client's. Through this difference the psychotherapist will gain a deeper understanding of the client in context. So Shaffer often consulted family and friends who knew the client well to facilitate therapy. Sometimes he brought this about indirectly. He would say "Examine the client and treat the family and friends." (Dorcus & Shaffer 1945)

Symptoms derive from solutions a client uses to help cope with their discomforts from their conflicts and problems. These solutions become patterned, habitual, and reinforced, since they bring some distraction and relief. Patterns begin with mild tendencies that become more complex and rigid over time. In the emotional setting of a positive and supportive therapeutic relationship, the client and therapist will discover together better ways, thereby reducing symptoms.

There are great varieties in the natural and learned abilities of individuals to work out positive adjustments to life. Disorders are the manifestations of a long series of processes that are in part hereditary, in part environmental compounded with the personal meanings given by the client. Complete understanding rests on examination of all of these factors, to discern the unique combination that characterizes the individual client.

EMPIRICAL OBSERVATION

Shaffer recognized the importance of the empirical sciences for clinical psychology. The key element of scientific inquiry is observation. But observation, especially in the realm of behaviors, can be very fallible. Think of the magician who carefully misdirects attention toward unimportant matters so that the important movements go unobserved. For psychologists in a clinical situation, unbiased observation may be difficult to achieve. Though the limitations of observation are many, Shaffer believed that good training of clinical psychologists should teach skills in observation and inference. (Review the skills Combs & Rogers taught in Part Three for further details.)

The psychotherapist learns to carefully follow observations. With experience, therapists develop the sensitivity to notice things that may not be obvious to the client, yet are important. The therapist's training analysis or personal therapy also helps to cultivate clarity of perception and freedom from distortions that can distract direct observation. The self-knowledge of the therapist helps in a subjective sense, to allow the personality of the therapist to become a useful part of observation.

Some phenomena are more available to our direct observation than others. This is where psychological testing has been invaluable in expanding psychological knowledge. The projective concept, used in projective testing of clients, relies upon the scientific assumption of clinical psychology, that behavior is psychically determined and thus expressive of inner dynamics. If clients are given something open-ended to react to, their reactions reveal much about their motivations. Psychologists develop models which attempt to make sense of human behavior based upon the combination of their theoretical hypotheses, which have been carefully tested with direct and indirect observation.

Areas inaccessible to simple observation and inference may also be clarified by experimentation. Experimental design has become far more diverse over the years using devices of measurement that are sensitive to the psychological element. Today, some psychologists who have a clinical practice may not personally involve themselves in research. But the findings of clinical studies that are published in the professional journals are available and can be helpful to improve therapeutic models and methods. Clinicians will discover links between research and practice which can be practically applied. Continual updating through learning insures this.

PART FIVE

GOALS OF PSYCHOTHERAPY

Even though the theories of psychotherapy may differ, the goals are always the same: "To secure the soundest degree of mental or psychological health" (Shaffer & Lazarus 1952, 297). This includes development of understandings, release of personal resources, and continual growth in social adjustment. Psychotherapy should help clients to make changes and grow so that their life situation can be met adequately.

Symptoms and complaints must be recognized as signposts. Clients may misjudge themselves as "stupid" because they are not making adequate use of their potentials. Their conflicts may prevent them from taking action. Once the barriers have been removed through the therapeutic process, these kinds of difficulties seem to melt away. Shaffer felt that one of the general goals of psychotherapy is to help people to know themselves more clearly so that they can make wiser choices.

One of Shaffer's own favorite, creative techniques which he developed and used at the Johns Hopkins Psychological Center was to have clients and students write out in detail their own autobiography. He found that this allowed them to observe their behaviors, thoughts, and feelings somewhat objectively, as a therapist might, yet at the same time from their own felt experience. One of his students wrote a five hundred-page autobiography! Most felt that the significance of their developmental experiences, motivations, and interpersonal relationships became clearer through the process of writing the autobiography.

THERAPEUTIC RELATIONSHIP

Since others have given up their attempts to help him and he himself is without hope, the new environment must provide hope. (Shaffer & Lazarus 1952, 304)

A universal truth for all effective therapy is the importance of the therapeutic relationship. Shaffer believed the essence of the relationship is not a physical environment but an emotional setting. How the relationship is handled distinguishes the good therapist from the bad. Therapy can take place anywhere, anytime. Setting is background.

The relationship should offer something new for the client. Frequently people come to therapy when they feel uncomfortable in their usual environment. They may have ambivalent relationships with friends and family, or they may not feel able to express themselves freely in their everyday life. The therapist offers a situation in which clients can feel accepted, cared for, and free to disclose themselves fully. We found this to be true in our own research, when comparing insight therapy to hypnotherapy correlated with hemisphere dominance. Intuitive, right-hemisphere dominant subjects did better with insight therapy. Rational left-hemisphere dominant subjects improved more with hypnosis. Each found the method offered them something new, filling deficits in their functioning. (Simpkins & Simpkins, 1983)

Shaffer was warm, supportive, responsive, and understanding as a therapist. He believed in being calm and reasonable yet firm, if needed. Therapy offers a new kind of relationship; a therapeutic one that is permissive and accepting of the client's thoughts and feelings, yet responsive to the situations of life. Not all behaviors must be accepted, and this is made clear to the client, but any thought or feeling is met with sympathetic interest. Clients should be made to feel comfortable enough to talk with the therapist. This depends upon the atmosphere of permissiveness and nonjudgmental attitude which the therapist creates in the session.

Shaffer believed that suggestion is present in all forms of therapy, therefore it should be deliberately and sincerely utilized. No intervention is entirely free of suggestion. Suggestion operates to influence responses even if the suggestion giver is unaware and unintentional in using it. Suggestion should be realistic and benevolent. The client's response is what defines it.

Recognizing the suggestive possibilities in the therapeutic relationship, the therapist can be a strong source of support. Another quality of suggestion is directing attention. Therapists can use suggestion to direct the client's attention toward the therapeutic process, carefully engaging the client's interest and involvement. Gradually, and almost seemingly without effort, the client may then begin improving without understanding or even quite knowing. After the change has taken effect, therapists can direct clients' attention toward the improvements they have accomplished but do not yet recognize. Later, when resistance may arise, the relationship established earlier helps in coping. Other uses involve such valuable experiences as alterations of perception to demonstrate that clients can have control over body functions similar to symptoms, and to show the influence in general of the mind over the body.

TYPES OF PSYCHOTHERAPY

Shaffer had a broad perspective concerning psychotherapy. Rather than narrowing into one approach he was able to draw from a number of different methods and make them blend well together. The different types of therapy are not mutually exclusive. Without realizing it in actual practice, most therapists draw from methods which lie outside of their therapeutic rationale. Shaffer chose to do this deliberately, thereby expanding the potential for strategic interventions.

PART FIVE

PSYCHOBIOLOGY: DISTRIBUTIVE ANALYSIS AND SYNTHESIS

> There is no doubt that we deal with a body of facts and methods
> that have a common ground and frame not completely handled by
> any one single "approach". There are many approaches used and
> at work.   (Meyer in Leif 1948, 551)

Shaffer's conception of therapy was influenced very deeply by Adolph
Meyer's (1866-1950) theory of psychobiology. Meyer developed an
approach to psychotherapy that treated clients in all facets of their life.
Psychobiology starts not from mind, body, or elements, but from the fact
that human beings are a unified whole. "We frankly recognize that there is
a functioning of the whole unit, of what we call the person" (Meyer 1951,
93)

Meyer's therapeutic philosophy of psychobiology is known as
distributive analysis and synthesis.   In this approach, simultaneous
emphasis is placed on all the relevant factors and situations of the client.
Treatment is guided by "The need to achieve a wholesome integration of
the total personality as well as of various functions" (Dorcus & Shaffer
1945, 489). Procedures are applied with a great deal of flexibility, so that
the therapist and client are able to respond to whatever potentially
therapeutic opportunities present themselves.

The influence of Adolf Meyer on the field of psychiatry was broad and
deep. He formulated the basic foundation that has become an accepted
standard for much of psychiatric treatment today. Meyer had brilliant
understandings of the human being and pointed in his psychobiology toward
treatment on an institutional scale. He left the practical application of
technique open to the practitioner.

Shaffer felt deeply in agreement with this view of interdependence
among the disciplines. He took the psychobiological orientation of Meyer
but improved and developed it further by incorporating specific
psychological methods applied with effective techniques for application.

AN ACTIVELY INTEGRATIVE APPROACH TO TREATMENT

> Certainly here is a method of treatment which offers the opportunity
> for utilization of all the psychotherapeutic procedures of known
> value. (Dorcus & Shaffer 1945, 488)

In general, analysis of the client with synthesis of the client's experience
is most effective. Clients can be assisted in modifying learned patterns of
response using desensitization and reeducation. Ideally, both insight and
support are interwoven. Support helps the client to handle analytic insights

and insights are more accessible in a supportive environment. Threat is automatically diminished in the safe atmosphere created.

Shaffer recognized the value of suggestion and used it therapeutically. Like Erickson, Shaffer was willing to utilize certain givens of human nature and personality. These qualities could help clients heal when properly channeled within the therapeutic relationship .

Therapists should take stock of individual differences and vary their approach to fit the client's needs. Distributive analysis gave an active role to therapists and encouraged clients to be active as well. Ultimately, clients must take the action necessary to make their lives satisfactory. At certain points in the therapeutic process, the client can be encouraged to make real changes. At these critical moments, the therapist can advise, guide, and assist clients to participate in some of the activities they may have avoided in the past.

Whenever analysis is used in therapy the purpose is to achieve an integrative synthesis of personality, situation, and responses in the life situation. Shaffer felt that analysis often spends a great amount of time and effort studying the failures of the client, without utilizing the client's successes. By taking the synthetic view, the therapist helps the client to make use of material uncovered in analysis by integrating it to bring about successful functioning both within the personality as well as in the personal world of the client. Every analysis should lead to synthesis, as the client finds practical use of each session's insights for constructive change.

This approach allows the client's difficulties to be treated as a whole. Analysis is distributed across the entire perceptual field. Inner and outer, personality and environment, are all seen as interrelated and interdependent, similar to Comb's view. Analysis includes assessing intelligence, personality, physical diagnosis, if relevant, social relationships and environment. Shaffer believed that the mature and experienced clinician could benefit from this open scheme for treatment. But experience and time are necessary to learn to apply these skills well. Distributive analysis gives the therapist a broad orientation for practice.

CAPACITY AND INTELLIGENCE

Shaffer had a great deal to say about intelligence. (Shaffer & Dorcus, 1945, Shaffer & Lazarus, 1952) Drawing from Hebb, Shaffer believed learning was primarily perceptual in nature. He held that cerebral function is not simply located in certain regions of one hemisphere: The brain is not a localized organ of functions. The nonlocalized use of the brain for functions in younger individuals permits the later transfer of capacity to other areas than would be expected. Later in life individuals may use and reconnect their functions creatively, as needed. Lost functions caused by brain damage, for example, can be regained through relearning and reeducation as other areas take over the functions fulfilled by the injured area. He thought it more likely that this is facilitated when other pathways were occasionally traversed before the switchover. He found support for this position in Lashley, Franz, and Pavlov's research. (Shaffer, 1968) This predates the research findings of Gazzaniga (1985) that some forms of brain damage do not result in permanent loss of function because the brain functions as a whole to compensate for lost areas. New mapping takes place as the brain forms new neural pathways to accommodate for what has been damaged. (Ramachandran, 1993)

Piaget's (1952) observations and experiments indicated that through the individual's reaction to and interaction with the environment, intelligence develops and changes. People go through a process of accommodation and assimilation. Developmental learnings gradually alter the structure of intelligence. This development occurs most rapidly during the first years of life. Early experiences can have a crucial effect on intelligence. Experiments show that children reared in orphanages where stimuli is limited compare poorly to children raised with greater environmental opportunities. The orphans' scores on various infant scales showed less maturity as well as less learning capacity than children raised by their parents. (Shaffer 1952)

Shaffer concluded, at a time when many people believed that intelligence was genetically fixed, that though bound somewhat by genetic givens, intelligence could be developed. Everyone can improve, regardless of their endowments. Learning is more powerful than genetics. Environmental stimuli, coupled with the brain's natural ability to adapt to limitations, can be used by psychotherapists to help people overcome problems. His use of many seemingly different methods of therapy derived from understanding of how the brain functions and how intelligence develops.

Personality Theories

Three important variables are emphasized by most psychotherapeutic approaches to a greater or lesser degree: the stimulus situation, an organism with certain characteristics, and the response. The stimulus and the response can be observed empirically, but the organism in between links the response to the stimulus in a consistent and enduring patterned way. This pattern is what Shaffer means by personality.

People have a certain structure to their personality. Theories of personality dynamics attempt to explain and predict human behavior from these dynamics. Personality theories offer the therapist a scientific way to understand the inner life of the client. All types of therapy rely upon a theory of personality even if it is not explicitly included, to help in developing the best treatment.

Shaffer interpreted personality broadly by integrating a variety of perspectives. He stated wisely, "The thing that is striking about all these theories is that the terminology differs but the concepts are quite similar." (Shaffer 1952, 204). He believed that it does not greatly matter what theory is used by the clinician, but considered it important to be familiar with the variety of points of view.

BEHAVIORAL THEORIES

The most extreme position of Watsonian behaviorism considered the personality to simply be: "The end product of our habit systems." (Shaffer and Lazarus, 1956) Later behaviorists frequently tended to view responses as attempts to reduce tensions or react to reward. Stimulus-response connections can become very complex and link to varied meanings. Biological, experiential , and cultural characteristics determine individual differences. Learned associations become generalized and more complex to include the richness of human personality. These generalized patterns constitute the individual's personality. More is needed to account for the range of human behavior. Other theories help.

TRAITS, TYPES, AND SYNDROMES

Trait theories of personality add complexity to the Stimulus-Organism-Response equation of the behaviorists. Allport referred to the S-O-R paradigm as "quasi-mechanical". He considered it the starting point of his theory but by no means comprehensive enough. Traits determined behavior, though not in a rigid sense. "The personality is not a fixed monolith, but rather a flexible, ever developing and evolving group of sets called traits, predispositions, preferred patterns, attitudes, personal characteristics, etc." (Allport 1961, 259)

In trait theories, all people have traits. Some traits are common to all people; others are unique to the individual. Traits affect and explain motivation and behavior. Motives are diverse. They can be transient or recurring, conscious or unconscious, tension reducing or tension creating. "About all we can say is that a person's motives include all that he is trying consciously or unconsciously, reflexively, or deliberately to do." (Allport 1961, 221)

Other theorists made distinctions based upon types. Shaffer felt that these distinctions are important since a type can be seen as a broader category usually including a number of traits. Sheldon's endomorph, ectomorph, and mesomorph are one of the commonly known type theories. Jung developed the concepts of introvert and extrovert. Traits and types can help the clinician predict how people will tend to act and respond in patterned ways. Shaffer believed that traits and types are especially useful when the behavior patterns they describe fit closely to the client's behavior. Traits and types offer a way to map the client's patterns of response for planning therapeutic interventions. But do not be limited by one map.

Syndromes and symptoms offer another way to categorize personality patterns. Syndromes, unlike some traits, are inadequate and incomplete means for fulfillment of motives. They represent the best attempt possible at the time. The clinician should develop a sense of the syndrome as the individual's personal expression involving maladjustment to their life. This position anticipated by fifty years the developments of the DSM, now used to classify disorders, syndromes and clusters of trait-tendencies. Combs and Rogers would subsume all of these motives under the master motive of fulfillment: self-actualization.

MURRAY'S NEED AND PRESS

Murray offered a complex but balanced motivational theory of personality. He conceived of motives as needs. He called stimuli from the environmental situation, press. Press and need are in a dynamic and complex interaction between the actual environment and the subjectively perceived environment.

> The representation of the personality as a hierarchical system of general traits or need complexes leaves out the nature of the environment, a serious omission. We must know to what circumstances an individual has been exposed. (Murray in Shneidman 1981, 183)

Needs act as a directing force behind behavior. Needs lead an individual to seek or avoid, attend or respond to certain kinds of press, but needs are a hypothetical process, inferred from behavior, within the individual. Press, according to Murray was also a phenomenal concept based on the personal frame of reference. How the stimulus situation is perceived determines its "press" nature.

The need-press aspect of any event represents a dynamic emotional-cognitive structure, called Thema. Themas involve not only the stimulus response relationships, but also the individual's perceptual field. Themas are never static, always the result of many forces acting simultaneously.

Murray applied his system for screening and selecting appropriate candidates for counterespionage and strategic service during World War Two. He succeeded and was awarded Legion of Merit for his work on this project.

PSYCHOANALYTICAL THEORY

Psychoanalytic theory revolves around mental dynamics, a motivational theory of forces or drives. Freud believed in two instincts or basic types of drives: the biological, physical needs and the psychological, Eros-life urge and Thanatos-death urge. Eros, or libido was the sexual urge. Thanatos represented the self-destructive urge. People will tend to avoid pain and

141

seek pleasure. However, any realistic look at most adults shows that we often put off our present enjoyment for a valued future objective. This behavior shows the working of the reality principle. Mental processes are the result of the interplay of all these forces.

Freud gave structure to inner dynamics with his now famous ego, superego, and id formulation. The ego mediates perceptions selectively, organizing and guiding the judgment and intelligence of the organism. Beneath the ego are the chaotic forces of the id. The id is the source of all instinctual impulses. The superego, the social moralizer, decides which impulses are acceptable and which are not. Behavioral problems result when there is conflict between the id, ego, and superego. Shaffer believed that no theory of personality attempted to be as detailed and include as many aspects into one framework. For this the theory has received both criticism and loyal acceptance. He believed clinicians often tend to use aspects of these theories as part of their practice.

FIELD THEORY

Field theory, pioneered by Lewin and developed further by many phenomenological and sociological thinkers considers the motivations and situations to which people respond from the subjective vantage point of the life space. Lewin construed his paradigm for personality as "hodology", a new kind of space geometry he called psychological space. Psychological space is the psychological environment, everything that has importance to the individual. Lewin set up a mathematical, geometrical, and physical paradigm for his theory of personality in order to make it possible to visualize with diagrams.

The motivational aspects of behavior are called forces. These forces have direction, to push an individual one way or another, represented by vectors. Valences are the objects, goals, and ways of achieving goals. There could be positive or negative valences, depending upon the forces at work. Barriers are characteristics of a situation, which could slow down or block the approach of an individual to a goal. Lewin's theory described the characteristics of the life-space including the forces, barriers, goals, regions, and valences. Regions consist of perceptual, cognitive, and motor systems, operating as tools in the service of the inner personal needs. Need systems are diagrammed by closed circles. The thickness and thinness of the walls indicate whether needs are met or thwarted.

Lewin's theory took into account the historical context in terms of causation. He conceptualized two kinds of causation: historical and systematic. Historical causation depends on the previous situation causing the present event to come into being. Systematic causation pertains to relationships of the situation at a given moment in time. Lewin felt that science could only deal with systematic causation. Psychology must also confine itself to instantaneous events. This, according to Shaffer, is a limitation in this perspective.

The phenomenological perspective includes aspects of gestalt and humanism in therapy. Combs and Snygg's statement of this theory was central. (See Part Three) The primary reference point for observation of human behavior is the individual phenomenal field. The phenomenal field is everything experienced by the individual at the moment of action. Learning is subsumed under the perceptual process of figure-ground differentiation. Our awareness is the figure in the foreground of perception. Everything else is background, the nonconscious.

When looked at together, the apparently different personality theories have similar concepts. Urges, drives, needs, forces, motives are all ways of identifying the motivational determinants of behavior. Although emphases differ, all systems deal with motivation (drive, urge, instinct, force, need), responses (actone, motoric, phenotypical traits, style, mechanism), and the stimulus situation in which or to which the organism responds (phenomenal field, life space, stimulus, press). Shaffer summarizes, "Given these three components organized in some fashion it is possible to describe everything that is found in all our present theories of personality" (Shaffer & Lazarus 1952, 205).

Each theory has strengths and weaknesses. The contributions of different theorists are complementary.

Psychological Tests Derive from Personality Theories

Shaffer assumed that personality is structured. From this structure, psychologists have been able to create psychological tests. David Rapaport's well-known work on psychological testing explains the projective procedure as the active and spontaneous structuring of material that reveals the person's structuring principles. Projective tests, used by psychologists to predict and classify, assume that the personality will manifest itself through the test.

> It is assumed that the psychological structure of the person is a principle governing all his behavior; and by vigorously applying this hypothesis one may succeed—more likely...in discovering some facets of the structure of a person in any of his life manifestations... (Rapaport, Gil & Schafer 1978, 225)

Measurement devices derive from the theoretical rationales of the various personality theories. Be familiar with the variety of points of view. Since theories lead to measurement devices, the clinician may find them useful along with their available test. For example, Murray's well-known Thematic Apperception Test (TAT) is based in his personality constructs. The Rorschach test discloses perceptual tendencies that are grounded in theories of personality such as psychoanalysis.

After clinicians are familiar with a measurement device, they sometimes use it without really knowing or subscribing to the theoretical assumptions behind that particular test. For example, many practitioners use the TAT without ever having actually read Murray's personality theory. Murray's TAT is widely used by clinicians in many ways, some quite different from how the author might have imagined. After administering the same test for many years, practitioners learn to recognize what typical responses are. This develops into an intuitive, normative sense that allows clients to be understood in relationship to the measure. By correlating a group of test results together, consistent patterns emerge.

TECHNIQUES OF PSYCHOTHERAPY
CATHARSIS

Techniques of psychotherapy are developed to help clients understand themselves better, to feel secure, and to be able to lead full and rewarding lives. One of the oldest techniques of psychotherapy is catharsis. The church has long employed this method in the form of confession. But secular catharsis is helpful as well. Emotionally meaningful therapeutic healing takes place through personal expression.

Catharsis can have many benefits if done correctly. Expressing material in a permissive and supportive atmosphere may reduce some of the pain and anxiety associated with the material. Verbalization of problems can also open up the possibility for people to look at themselves from varying perspectives.

The therapist must be careful not to push a client into catharsis. Problems are frequently associated with feelings of intense shame. People feel reluctance to discuss these matters and worry about what might happen if they did. Often people will try to attribute their problems to other causes such as overwork or physical disabilities. The therapist must not be too eager to accept superficial excuses. On the other hand, real environmental stressors should not be ignored. For these reasons, therapists should be careful not to push clients before they are ready. Once people feel the safety, trust, and support of a positive therapeutic relationship, they will naturally express their deeper feelings without prodding from the therapist.

How therapists handle these revelations varies with their therapeutic model. For example, directive style therapists will participate more actively than the nondirective style. What matters most in managing the early part of the catharsis is that the therapist can encourage free expression of feelings. Creating an atmosphere favorable to expressing and accepting the full range of emotions is essential.

Find the best balance between encouraging the client to express these feelings without going beyond the client's point of tolerance. Shaffer felt that knowing just how far to go develops with experience and is the mark of a good therapist. Clinical judgment must be exercised.

Rapport is the central feature necessary for a successful catharsis. The therapist must allow time for the client to recognize the rapport, to experience the therapist's understanding, tolerance and uncritical attitude.

Catharsis in and of itself can be therapeutic, but is best when combined with genuine understanding of the development of personality. Intellectual insight without a felt experience concerning inner dynamic to go along with it is usually not helpful.

The therapist must understand the personal meaning of the life experiences for the client. This helps to unravel how the client became disturbed. These experiences are related to each other. Symptoms represent acquired patterns. The therapist can look for similar patterns and trace out how the reactions may have first begun and developed into fixed reaction patterns. Shaffer believed that older patterns, especially those established back in early childhood, tend to increase the feeling of insecurity for the client in the present. These usually need to be expressed during catharsis.

> The properly handled catharsis may, therefore, be said to be one in which the therapist has succeeded in getting the client to discuss his life experiences intimately and thus discharge emotional tensions, reveal unconscious attitudes, provide the basis for objectivity and perspective, and to experience a satisfactory and secure interpersonal relationship in the face of these revelations. (Shaffer & Lazarus, 1952 521)

DESENSITIZATION AND REEDUCATION

Shaffer's approach to psychotherapy dealt with as many areas of the person's life as necessary or possible. Treatment involved inner and outer work, including insight and catharsis, medical treatment if relevant, as well as assistance with the client's environment. Desensitization and reeducation can bring about change in social interactions and affect emotional reactions to real-life situations.

Desensitization helps people become more comfortable in the face of emotionally charged situations. Reeducation involves the retraining of habits of response. The two processes are interdependent and work most effectively when used together.

People react differently. A situation experienced as traumatic to one person may not be experienced as traumatic to another. Certain types of life circumstances may feel threatening because they are associated in a client's mind with an earlier painful experience. Through the intervening years, the individual develops beliefs based on earlier experiences and continues to misinterpret many situations as similar to the trauma. This becomes cemented into patterned responses, falling outside of awareness and usually expressed as symptoms. According to Meyer, these patterns have all the characteristics of habits which he called "habit patterns of reaction". Most mental disturbances involve either evading an uncomfortable memory of the primary experience or trying to avoid experiencing anything like it in the present. These habits are fixed and not subject to reality testing.

Desensitization guides people to face and experience the painful experience repeatedly but in a modified way so that it can be tolerated. Eventually, the painful edge to the experience is softened and the client begins to feel less and less threatened. Shaffer believed that desensitization takes two tracks. One is aimed at desensitization of the symptom, which is the outer manifestation of the problem. The other is to discover and desensitize the origin of the problem.

In actual practice this technique usually involves the client imaginatively going through the situation with the therapist in the therapeutic session. The therapist and client discuss the situation, going over the various aspects, looking at it from different perspectives. Clients express themselves about the problem over and over, which in itself has a therapeutic effect. The meaning of the situation gradually becomes disengaged from the originally traumatic experience as it is expressed repeatedly in the nonthreatening milieu of the therapeutic session.

Modern exposure therapy uses this principle by helping people confront their trauma in a safe, supportive situation. For example, imagine a young child who has never met a ferocious dog. Innocently, he pets the dog and is badly frightened when the dog bites him. Following this the child becomes intensely afraid of dogs. Desensitization through exposure therapy would involve bringing the child into the presence of friendly dogs. While supporting the child emotionally the therapist helps the child to pet a dog without any adverse reactions from the animal.

Mental disturbances may not be as concrete as this example. Often the client has no specific situation to physically visit, in order to overcome the problem. However, desensitization takes place through an imaginative reexperiencing in the presence of the therapist.

Reeducation begins when the client feels less threatened and includes retraining habits of response regarding the problem. Sometimes this actually requires educating the client to fill deficits.

First clients must recognize that they have a difficulty. Clients are frequently brought to therapy by family and friends who feel more bothered than the client. Until the client wishes to do something about it, reeducation will not be effective. Clients must gain the self-confidence that they can tackle the difficulty with the therapist's help. As Frank emphasized, faith in the process is paramount to all forms of therapy. Successful therapy engenders faith.

Reeducation involves informing clients, perhaps sharing with them statistics about how common their problem might be. In drug and alcohol rehabilitation, for example, this is a common practice. Once people learn what is known about their problems, they can face them. Then they can take responsibility for resolving them. The therapist encourages and assists in formulating some tangible, practical plan to help. By working together a mature perspective becomes possible.

ENLISTING RATIONAL THINKING

Dubois (1907) and Dejerine (1913) developed persuasion as a method of therapy. Their therapeutic systems were dependent upon persuasion as the main agent of change. They believed that people should develop critical mindedness and a sense of independence. Rational use of their intellect will make the difference. They coached people about bad mental habits and false ideas that led to their symptoms. Although therapies of today do not rely wholly on persuasion, many of the cognitive therapies such as Ellis's Rational Emotive Therapy and Beck's Cognitive Therapy have their roots in this approach.

Other factors outside the theory contribute to the method, helping it succeed. The therapist appeals indirectly to the emotions by using reason and logic. Unconscious factors are built on, and emotional support is given indirectly. "In persuasive therapy, the client gets well because he has been convinced that there is no reason he should not" (Shaffer & Lazarus 1952, 327).

Shaffer believed that persuasion can be very helpful for minor problems if done correctly. Unskilled therapists may misuse persuasion by trying to impose the therapist's will upon the client. The best use of these methods is to work on patterns of meaning and belief, so the client is inspired to take on changes in behaviors, attitudes, or emotional response. Cognitive therapy takes the most useful aspects of the persuasive approach and develops them further by enlisting cognitive processing to face and resolve irrational thinking.

THE THERAPEUTIC USE OF SUGGESTION AND HYPNOSIS

Psychotherapists should use every effective therapeutic method available. Hypnosis is a valuable therapeutic method to help with any form of therapy. Just as Erickson used mechanisms of mind for suggestion and hypnosis, Shaffer used hypnosis and suggestion as mechanisms of therapy.

One useful application of hypnosis is for symptom removal. When the symptoms are so disabling as to block all psychotherapeutic efforts, it may be necessary to remove symptoms before therapy can be attempted. The mastery, confidence, and relief gained from the hypnotic experience helps clients face further treatment gracefully and courageously. Sometimes, removing a symptom is sufficient. Other times, more comprehensive therapy should be done, which can use hypnosis alone or in combine with other methods. Hypnotic work can provide additional emotional support and positive resources along the way.

Memory can be enhanced in hypnosis, making it an effective tool for recovering helpful material from past experiences for insight. But modern therapists are reluctant to try to recover memories by hypnosis. Expectancy and bias can affect client material leading to false memories. Therapists should keep this in mind and consider recovered memories as subjective experience.

Hypnosis can also be used to supplement desensitization therapy. Traumatic material can be reexperienced in hypnosis without the corresponding anxiety and distress. This begins the desensitization process. Conditioning and learning may also be enhanced.

Hypnosis can be performed with either a directive or nondirective, permissive approach. Primary in deciding how to approach the situation is to take into account the individuality of the client. For some, a strong authoritative prescription for change through hypnotic trance is very powerful in bringing positive outcome. Other clients who wish to participate more actively prefer suggestions that are presented in such a way that they can choose to accept those which are helpful and reject all others. Indirect suggestions, as Erickson so expertly demonstrated, give clients the opportunity to make their own meaningful associations and links.

When active client participation is being used with hypnosis, it is helpful to demonstrate the influence the mind has over the body. Clients can be led to experiment personally with hypnotic phenomena such as anesthesia of a hand or paralysis of an arm to directly experience how the mind can affect the body. Vivid illustrations are fascinating and help clients to understand how their symptoms are often created unintentionally by the suggestions they give to themselves without knowing. Such learnings become the stepping stones to disentangle from neurotic patterns. Suggestion can be an ally for change, part of the synthesis. All methods then work together for the benefit of the client.

Conclusions

Shaffer had an open mind and engendered openness in all who knew him, as students, clients, and colleagues. When working in therapy he was always ready to expand his approach to meet the individual's needs. His kindly, supportive warmth and truly broad-based knowledge of therapy can be an inspiration to all who embark on the helping path. Many great practitioners today continue on the same path he walked, aiming for the most effective results. New methods and variations of classical approaches are evolving.

PART FIVE

Chapter Fifteen

Synthesis in Application

Shaffer used distributive analysis and synthesis as a flexible, open-ended approach that can incorporate any accepted therapeutic methods as part of treatment. A complete and thorough understanding of clients and their perceptual field should be your guide for applying a particular method. Careful interviewing and assessment when needed will aid the therapist in decisions about treatment strategy.

Shaffer used the case history to guide him, like the one delineated in Part Two on Whitehorn. Diagnosis is the second means of evaluation. But diagnosis may not give precise information about the form of therapy to follow. Shaffer felt that diagnostic labels merely offer general descriptions of the client's symptoms and processes. We can classify together clients with superficially similar types of problems. But the same symptoms do not necessarily develop from the same circumstances and do not necessarily require the same treatment. Shaffer's system for classification was much more practical and individualized.

Following the interview, ask yourself the following questions:

1. What is the capacity of the client to profit from psychotherapy? This includes intelligence, age, and resources. Intelligence tests can be used, but remember that intelligence can be developed somewhat, depending upon the nature of the problem.

2. What tensions and forces led to this client's action? This is where the different theories of personality become useful. We have outlined some of the theories which Shaffer drew from to explain why people act the way they do. Use your own theoretical framework for personality and motivation to answer this question. This includes the perceptual field approach.

3. What are the individual ways this client adjusts to frustrations and conflicts? Simply discovering conflicts and motivations that are responsible for a person's behavior are not enough to understand the client fully. Individual differences account for what makes one person break down in crisis while another does not. How people learn to cope with adversity tells us how they adjust to life. Analyze how your client adjusts or copes with conflicts.

This question may also be answered differently depending on your theoretical framework. You may prefer to use character mechanisms and interpersonal dynamics of defense, such as rationalization, or projection, typical categories of psychoanalysis. Or from a perceptual psychology perspective, search for personal meaning, expressed through the self-actualization tendency. How is this client not fulfilling him or herself?

4. What is the client's presenting problem, and how does this problem fit into the context of the person as a whole? Include many factors, such as personal history, environmental influences, constitution, and emotional factors.

THE AUTOBIOGRAPHY

One of the best ways to get a personal report from the client is by developing what Shaffer called a biographical analysis. The biographical analysis may be done through the interview, as we have discussed earlier. But Shaffer often used an alternative: the autobiography. One of the many values in this self-report is the free expression of personal meanings. And a great deal of time is saved for the clinician, since clients can write their autobiography at home, in their spare time. People can freely edit and contemplate, thereby reducing threat. The report is done in the client's own language, in ways that make sense personally. The technique requires that the client be somewhat literate and intelligent. The clinician can gain an excellent sense of the client from the autobiography.

Many psychologists have praised the importance of a thorough case history for truly understanding the client. Lewin (1926) said that the study of the individual case is the only method of evolving a non-Aristotelian science of behavior (Shaffer 1952, 79). The autobiography can be an important tool for understanding the perceptual field.

As a clinician, you might find it helpful for developing your self-awareness to carefully write out your own autobiography. This will help you to have a more empathetic understanding of the process experienced by your client and add a deeper understanding of your own dynamics.

DIRECTIONS FOR AUTOBIOGRAPHY

Write your autobiography. Include the following: family history, personal background, school and college history, major experiences, aims and aspirations, and estimate of yourself and the world. When you have finished writing, read over the biography and add whatever information you omitted in your original statement.

INTERPRETATION OF THE AUTOBIOGRAPHY

Look for themes that repeat at various points in the autobiography. According to distributive analysis, these themes can be an important source of information for your work with the client.

The chief safeguard against error in analyzing the autobiographical statement is to consider all data regardless of your therapeutic bias. For example, an analyst might interpret rigid toilet training as the root of an individual's later problems. In another case where the parents were divorced when the client was nine, this might be interpreted as a major influence on problems. Anyone who is not a psychoanalyst might find it easy to criticize the first case interpretation as biased. More therapists might have difficulty noticing any bias in the second interpretation. Many thousands of healthy people come from divorced families. Hold your interpretations tentatively until more is known. Consider your interpretations as hypotheses instead. You may adapt Whitehorn's triangulation technique to this: seek convergence.

We use a combination of experience, common sense, and our personal grasp of psychological theories to interpret the autobiography. As you gain more experience, you will begin to notice patterns among different clients. From these trends you can make predictions. Do not be afraid to use common sense. All of the psychotherapists presented in this book held common sense in high esteem. Common sense can always be checked against your psychological theory to help you understand the subtler forces driving behavior.

DISCOVERING THE THEMES

Certain themes begin to emerge. Cross reference the themes over the many areas you have observed from the interview, autobiography, and intuition you have. If you are performing deep therapy, the theme you look for will be comprehensive, covering many aspects of functioning. If you are doing short-term, limited work, follow a theme that is directly related to the target area.

You can also apply your particular therapeutic orientation to a distributive analysis. For example, a cognitive therapist could think about repeating mental constructions and analyze broader themes from particular issues to discern thinking patterns that are bringing about the problem.

You do not have to limit your scope to conscious analysis. Therapists like Erickson, Combs, and Rogers used their intuitive and unconscious understandings to evoke themes. Let yourself become sensitive to implications and subtle references. We have described this use of therapeutic intuition in Parts Three and Four. Ideally you will combine all of your therapeutic tools to uncover the central themes.

Keep in mind that your analysis should be elastic and open-ended. No principle is absolute, even the assumption that you will find a common theme. Shaffer cautioned practitioners not to assume anything. Let the individual client be your ultimate guide.

WHEN TO USE DIFFERENT METHODS

Psychotherapists need a variety of clinical methods. All the general categories offered, such as reassurance, suggestion, hypnosis, catharsis, desensitization and reeducation are available. Also, modern psychology has developed new ones. However, keep in mind that technique is secondary to the relationship and therapeutic interaction. Shaffer used many methods with his clients, yet he always maintained a strong therapeutic relationship. He recognized that methods without the relationship are a mere hollow shell.

If you would like to expand your repertoire of methods, your task is twofold: first you must learn to perform the techniques associated with each method and second, you must know when to apply them. The answer to the first part of this is found in many books that detail methods and techniques. The reader is encouraged to consult our bibliography as well as other modern texts for sources on the different methods. The second part, when to apply them, is less often available and therefore is included here, in general categories of methods.

REASSURANCE AND SUGGESTION

Clients come to therapy hopeful and expectant that the therapist can help them to do what they have failed to do on their own. The therapist is in an excellent position to use suggestion successfully. The skillful use of suggestion can facilitate the therapeutic process.

Assess the client's attitudes coming into therapy. This will tell you whether the client seems open to suggestion. You can use suggestion throughout treatment to encourage the client's efforts, if you feel sincerely in accord. Suggestion works best when founded on truth.

Reassurance can be used when the client is extremely anxious, when there is a danger that the client will act out. These techniques can also have uses with very weak, wavering individuals or compulsive clients. Reassurance can also be an important part of brief therapy where the client does not have the financial or psychological resources to make deep-seated changes.

People sometimes feel incapable and inadequate. Suggestion can help to mobilize talents and capacities that might be helpful for combating their problems. For example, an anxious client may feel unable to relax, but you can suggest that there have been some times in her life when she felt very comfortable, and invite her to remember a particular time. As Whitehorn said, it is important to use the assets clients bring into the therapeutic situation. Suggestion is one way to stimulate these abilities to start working for them. Erickson always looked for the resources and helped his patients unlearn their limitations. Combs and Rogers helped clients clarify their feelings and find better meanings, to give them access to resources they did not know they had. Many perspectives of the situation are possible.

DESENSITIZATION AND REEDUCATION

Desensitization is useful for overcoming excessive sensitivities, such as feelings of inadequacy, shyness, and fears. Contemporary therapy has a number of effective methods for circumscribed problems such as individual and social phobias and panic attacks. All of these approaches help the client to become less sensitive to the disturbing stimulus, thereby preventing the emotional and physiological reactions that are part of their discomfort. Desensitization can also be helpful when you do not expect the client to be able to rationally or consciously understand the problem, but you believe the client would be better without it.

Reeducation offers training in new behaviors, attitudes and feelings—new possibilities to help people actualize the change brought about from desensitization. You can guide the client in practicing situations, inform them about possible circumstances they will encounter, and educate them to help them cope in the future.

Without reeducation, the client might not be able to sustain therapeutic changes. Reeducation also helps with changes that have taken place through other methods, such as suggestion, hypnosis, reassurance, and catharsis.

EXPRESSING EMOTIONS: CATHARSIS

Catharsis is part of most forms of therapy even though the ways it is used will vary. Many therapists agree that some form of expressing conflict material is essential for therapeutic results, although there are exceptions. If your approach includes catharsis, you need to know when to allow it and how to handle it.

The extent to which catharsis can be used successfully depends upon a secure therapeutic relationship. Your client must feel comfortable enough with you to share painful or embarrassing experiences. Airing feelings in a permissive and accepting atmosphere will help reduce anxiety. In the context of a positive, supportive therapeutic relationship, clients can reconsider uncomfortable feelings, thoughts, beliefs, and behaviors. Catharsis can be used to provide support and increase trust. Being listened to without judgment can be very therapeutic for clients who have had difficulties in their interpersonal relationships.

When guiding clients through expressing feelings allow them to express themselves freely. Catharsis can help lessen fears and guilt feelings that are inappropriate. Often the client will find that once disturbing feelings are recognized and expressed in therapy, they take on a less threatening character. This is well illustrated by a client of the authors who had frightening recurring nightmares of monsters chasing her. At first she found it very difficult to even describe the dreams. As she gradually began to talk about them, angry emotions came out. She was very surprised to realize that her monsters were her own anger. In the true safety and support of the relationship, she analyzed the meaning. She accepted her angry feelings, considered their meaning in the context of her values along with other more loving and positive feelings toward people in her life. Then she could consider and develop more mature ways to respond to her circumstances and resolve her conflicts with others. The nightmares stopped.

154

WORKING UNCONSCIOUSLY WITH HYPNOSIS

Hypnosis is a useful adjunct to many forms of therapy or a complete therapeutic method in itself. The therapist must feel comfortable with this method and must be suitably trained in this method. A wide variety of resources are available such as the Erickson Institute, as mentioned earlier.

Hypnosis is very helpful with reduction of unnecessary tension. Sometimes tension makes it impossible for the client to even begin to do therapy. Skillful use of relaxation techniques in trance may encourage the tense client to continue coming to therapy as relief and resolution become a real experience, not just a wish. Even if the relief is temporary, the therapeutic value is immeasurable. As Frank's research demonstrates, these momentary vacations from symptoms are very real and comforting. Such moments raise expectancy and faith in therapy, an important part of the process, setting the wheels of change in motion.

Hypnosis can strengthen the therapeutic relationship. Hypnosis gives clients something concrete to do. As clients practice going in and out of trance, new abilities develop. The therapist gives the client new and useful tools for handling discomforts. This helps to bolster confidence in the power of the therapeutic method and raise clients' confidence in themselves. A strong bond often develops between therapist and client. During the final session, the authors asked a client who had suffered from anxiety what she found most helpful about therapy. She said, "Hypnosis!" Hypnosis had been used regularly, along with other therapeutic methods including all the ones Shaffer mentioned. But to her, hypnosis was the most useful.

Hypnotic trance works directly with the unconscious mind, allowing clients to bypass conscious limits. Trance also enhances the client's capacity to cope better by using these skills. Potentials for self-actualizing may become a reality with the aid of the trance experience.

INTRODUCING HYPNOSIS TO YOUR CLIENT

If you would like to use hypnosis with a client, make sure the client feels comfortable with the idea. You may need to answer typical questions about hypnosis. People usually ask whether it is safe. You can confidently reassure them that a great deal of research supports that hypnosis in therapy with a qualified professional is safe.

BEGINNING WITH SUGGESTION

Shaffer liked to give clients a sample of unconscious functioning using suggestion. You can introduce your client to suggestion using direct suggestion. Tell your client, "Clasp your hands together. Imagine that your hands become stuck together and can-

not be separated. Enjoy the interesting experience."

Indirect suggestions are more open-ended. Have clients place their hands lightly on their knees and close their eyes. Then say, "You could wonder which hand would become lighter. Which one heavier? Perhaps your unconscious would like to have a different experience such as warmth or coolness. Wait with open curiousity." Spontaneous responses are fascinating and fun.

Experimenting with suggestion can help you to know how your client will do with hypnosis. Generally, people who are imaginative and willing to be experimental with their experiencing will find hypnosis useful.

CREATIVE SYNTHESIS

During the therapeutic process clients make discoveries and come to new understandings. These new understandings must be worked through so that they will become integrated into day to day living. This integrative process is what Shaffer meant by synthesis.

Therapy closes the gap between difficulties and potential assets. It is just as much a matter of actualizing potentials as it is resolving problems. Of course the client's complaints should not be minimized, but as Erickson so aptly pointed out, the original problem is not necessarily the true difficulty. Synthesis brings the client to fuller functioning that enlists abilities.

Notice the assets your client has. Sometimes clients overlook their assets. They may even consider these qualities to be deficits. Keep an open mind about all behaviors, feelings, or thoughts. You may find that what seems like a problem becomes an asset when viewed from another perspective. For example, we had a client who suffered from severe self doubt. He felt he was inferior partly because of his personal interpretation of his ethnic identity. His wife was disturbed that he was not a serious person. She felt that he always made fun of important matters. We worked with him in therapy to discover how his ability to take things lightly was an asset. He learned to apply humor to his inferiority feelings and take his experienced failings more lightly. By redirecting his sense of humor productively, he found a more fulfilling synthesis. He accepted himself and became more comfortable with his ethnic background. The change was recognized at work where he was given more and more responsibility. Eventually, the company sent him all over the world to handle negotiations with foreign companies.

Encouraging clients to accept themselves, even with those qualities they consider negative, is an important step toward transformation. Inner change begins to happen. Old situations are experienced differently. Feelings, thoughts, and behaviors alter as a result.

DIRECT, INDIRECT, AND NONDIRECT

Synthesis can be done throughout treatment. Some time should be devoted to synthesis at various times during therapy. Analysis should always be followed by synthesis. This facilitates working through the insights and understandings the client has discovered along the way, as new potential becomes available.

Directive methods are usually used in the early stages of therapy to guide the client along the lines that seem most relevant and productive based upon the analysis. Honest discussion of themes and new possibilities can be given to the client for consideration. Therapists may even point out links. But direction can only point the way. The client is discouraged from being dependent and encouraged to think things through. The therapist and client work together as collaborators. By the ending phases of therapy clients make connections for themselves. Inner work takes place within. At the close of therapy, clients will have made their own meaningful integration.

Indirect methods work differently. The therapist communicates in a manner that suggest possibilities to encourage a general direction. Exactly how the client will respond is left open, usually pointing inwards toward potential resources. For example, an indirect method could involve talking generally about making connections when you believe it will help your client to start putting together understandings.

Nondirective methods, as shown by Rogers and Combs, follow the client's line of inquiry, adding and reflecting only when it will clarify feelings and meanings. Be careful not to interject your own opinions as this might take the client away from the thread of deeper experiencing. Answers to the therapist's questions should require the client to discover how personal patterns and significant meanings interrelate.

Apply whichever method or methods you are most

comfortable with using. However, keep in mind that technique is secondary to the relationship and therapeutic intent. Deeper therapeutic understandings can happen within a strong therapeutic relationship. Methods without the relationship are a mere hollow shell. Let your unconscious help. Trust the intelligence within.

Conclusion

Timeless teachings left behind
Light the darkness
In the depths of the mind

The wellspring of psychotherapy is a source shared by all true healers of the mind. Theory is a springboard; technique propels the leap of faith into unknown waters of change and transcendence. Though these masters of the art may have different backgrounds, theoretical orientations, and degrees, they share a common root in the benevolence of the profession and lifelong personal commitment to help others.

Frank's research uncovered the nonspecific factors of hope, faith, trust, relationship, and therapeutic theory. Shaffer's approach revealed that methods are both specific and nonspecific. When you use a specific method well, you activate nonspecific processes common to all successful therapeutic change. Whitehorn taught that people function better and feel happier when they are treated with dignity, caring, and attention to their positive resources. Combs and Rogers taught that the person changes and meanings transform as life is fulfilled in accord with the true self. Erickson's teachings showed how to activate positive learning and change in the patient through therapeutic trance.

Even though all methods can be effective, certain methods are better for some problems, clients, or perhaps some therapists. Knowing when to use one method or another is helped by looking at the whole person in the total context.

Seek your inner wisdom as your guide. Inner wisdom will unite with the findings from external research and study, as you follow the noble calling of psychotherapy. Keep an open mind, apply what you know flexibly and sensitively, and always be willing to learn.

* * *

May the light of these timeless teachings shine brightly on your
path to help on your personal journey to mastery.

Bibliography

Allport, Gordon W. 1961. *Pattern and Growth in Personality*. New York: Holt, Rinehart and Winston.

Alexander, Franz G. & Sheldon T. Selesnick. 1966. *The History of Psychiatry*. New York: Harper and Row, Publishers.

American Translation of the official Chinese paramedical manual. 1977. *A Barefoot Doctor's Manual*. Philadelphia, Pennsylvania: Running Press.

Bandler, Richard & John Grinder. *Patterns of the Hypnotic Techniques of Milton H. Erickson, MD*. 1975. Cupertino, California: Meta Publications. Vol. I & II.

Benson, Herbert. 1975. *The Relaxation Response*. New York: William Morrow & Co.

Cantril, Hadley. 1950. *The Why of Man's Experience*. New York: Macmillan.

Combs, Arthur W. 1989. *A Theory of Therapy: Guidelines for Counseling Practice*. Newbury Park, California: Sage.

_____, & D. L. Avila, & W. W. Purkey. 1971. *Helping Relationships: Basic Concepts for the Helping Professions*. Boston: Allyn & Bacon.

_____, Ann Cohen Richards, & Fred Richards. 1976. *Perceptual Psychology: A Humanistic Approach to the Study of Persons*. New York: Harper & Row.

_____, & Donald Snygg. 1959. *Individual Behavior: A Perceptual Approach to Behavior*. New York: Harper & Row.

Dorcus, Roy M. 1956. *Hypnosis and its Therapeutic Applications*. New York: McGraw-Hill Book Company, Inc.

_____. & G. Wilson Shaffer. 1945. *Textbook of Abnormal Psychology*. Baltimore: The Williams & Wilkins Company.

Dohrenwend, Barbara Snell & Bruce P. Dohrenwend. 1984. *Stressful Life Events and Their Contexts*. Vol. II. New Brunswick, New Jersey: Rutgers University Press.

_____. & D. L. Crandall. 1970. Psychiatric symptoms in community, clinic, and mental hospital groups. *American Journal of Psychiatry*. 126: 1611-21.

_____. & B. Link. 1980. Formulation of hypotheses about the true prevalence of demoralization in the United States. *Mental Illness in the United States: Epidemiological Estimates*. ed. Dohrenwend. New York: Praeger. 114-32.

Erickson, Milton H. & Ernest L. Rossi. 1981. *Experiencing Hypnosis: Therapeutic Approaches to Altered States*. New York: Irvington Publishers, Inc.

_____. & _____. 1980. *The Nature of Hypnosis and Suggestion: The Collected Papers of Milton H. Erickson on Hypnosis*. Vol. I. New

York: Irvington Publishers, Inc.

_____. & _____. 1980. *Hypnotic Alteration of Sensory, Perceptual and Psychophysiological Processes*: *The Collected Papers of Milton H. Erickson on Hypnosis*. Vol. II. New York: Irvington Publishers, Inc.

_____. & _____. 1980. *Hypnotic Investigation of Psychodynamic Processes : The Collected Papers of Milton H. Erickson on Hypnosis*. Vol. III. New York: Irvington Publishers, Inc.

_____. & _____. 1980. *Innovative Hypnotherapy: The Collected Papers of Milton H. Erickson on Hypnosis*. Vol. IV. New York: Irvington Publishers, Inc.

_____. & _____. 1979. *Hypnotherapy: An Exploratory Casebook*. New York: Irvington Publishers, Inc.

_____. _____. & Sheila I. Rossi. 1976. *Hypnotic Realities: The Induction of Clinical Hypnosis and Forms of Indirect Suggestion.* New York: Irvington Publishers, Inc.

_____. 1966. The interspersal hypnotic technique for symptom correction and pain control. *American Journal of Clinical Hypnosis.* 3: 198-209.

_____. 1964. Initial experiments investigating the nature of hypnosis. *American Journal of Clinical Hypnosis*. 7: 254-57.

_____. 1964. The confusion technique in hypnosis. *American Journal of Clinical Hypnosis* 6: 183-207.

Farber, B. A. & J. D. Geller. 1977. Student attitudes toward psychotherapy. *Journal of American College Health Association*. 25:301-7.

Fiedler, F. E. 1950. The concept of an ideal therapeutic relationship. *Journal of Consulting Psychology*. 14: 239-45.

Frank, Jerome D. & Julia B. Frank. 1991 *Persuasion and Healing*. Baltimore: The Johns Hopkins University Press.

_____. 1986. Psychotherapy: The transformation of meanings. *Journal of the Royal Society of Medicine*. 79: 341-46.

_____. 1981. Holistic medicine: A view from the fence. *Johns Hopkins Medical Journal*. 149: 222-27.

_____. 1978. *Psychotherapy and the Human Predicament: A Psychosocial Approach*. New York: Schocken Books.

_____. Rudolf Hoehn-Saric, Stanley D. Imber, Bernard L. Liberman, Anthony R. Stone. 1978. *Effective Ingredients of Successful Psychotherapy*. New York: Brunner/Mazel.

_____. 1975. The faith that heals. Commencement Address at the Johns Hopkins University School of Medicine, May 23.

_____. 1975. Therapeutic Components of Psychotherapy. *Das Medizinische Prisma.* Germany: Boehringer Ingelheim. 2: 75.

_____. 1974. How psychotherapy heals. *Henry Ford Hospital Medical Journal*. 22:71-80.

_____. 1974. Psychotherapy: The restoration of morale. *American Journal of Psychiatry*. 131: 271-274.

_____. 1970. Psychotherapists need theories. *International Journal of*

BIBLIOGRAPHY

Psychiatry. 9:146-49.

Freud, Sigmund. 1953. *The Complete Psychological Works of Sigmund Freud.* ed. and translated by J. Strachey. Toronto: Hogarth Press.

Friedman, H. J. 1963. Patient expectancy and symptom reduction. *Arch. Gen. Psychiatry*. 8: 61-67.

Gazzaniga, M. S. 1985. *The Social Brain: Discovering the Networks of the Mind.* New York: Basic Books.

Gillespie, R. D. 1942. *Psychological Effects of War on Citizen and Soldier.* New York: W. W. Norton.Haley, Jay. Ed. 1985.

Haley, Jay. 1985. *Conversations with Milton H. Erickson, M.D.: Changing Individuals.* Vol. I. New York: Triangle Press.

_____. 1973. *Uncommon Therapy: The Psychiatric Techniques of Milton H. Erickson, M.D.* New York: W. W. Norton & Company, Inc.

_____. Ed. 1967. *Advanced Techniques of Hypnosis and Therapy: Selected Papers of Milton H. Erickson, M.D.* New York: Grune & Stratton.

_____. 1963. *Strategies of Psychotherapy.* New York: Grune & Stratton.

Hilgard, Ernest R. & Bower, Gordon H. 1975. *Theories of Learning.* Englewood Cliffs, New Jersey: Prentice-Hall, Inc.

Hull, Clark. 1933. *Hypnosis and Suggestibility: An Experimental Approach.* New York: Appleton-Century-Crofts, Inc.

Janet, Pierre. 1925. *Psychological Healing.* London: George Allen & Unwin Ltd. Vols. I & II

Kellner, R. & B. F. Sheffield. 1973.The one-week prevalence of symptoms in neurotic patients and normals. *American Journal of Psychiatry*. 130: 102-5.

Kilpatrick, Franklin P. ed. 1961. *Explorations in Transactional Psychology.* New York: New York University Press.

Kluckholn, Clyde and Henry A. Murray. 1964. *Personality in Nature, Society, and Culture.* New York: Alfred A. Knopf.

Koch, Sigmund. ed. 1959. *Psychology: A Study of a Science.* Vol II. New York: McGraw-Hill Book Company.

Kubie, Lawrence. 1975. *Neurotic Distortion of the Creative Process.* New York: Noonday Press.

Lazarus, Arnold. 1989. *The Practice of Multimodal Therapy: Systematic, Comprehensive, and Effective Psychotherapy.* Baltimore: Johns Hopkins University Press.

LeShan, Lawrence. 1974. *The Medium, the Mystic, and the Physicist: Toward a General Theory of the Paranormal.* New York: Viking Press.

Lief, Alfred. 1948. *The Commonsense Psychiatry of Dr. Adolf Meyer.* New York: McGraw-Hill Book Company, Inc.

Mullen, J. & N. Abeles. 1972. Relationship of liking, empathy, and therapist's experience to outcome of therapy. *Psychotherapy, 1971, an Aldine Annual.* Chicago: Aldine-Atherton.

Orlinsky D. E. & K. J. Howard. 1980. Gender and psychotherapeutic outcome. *Women and Psychotherapy*. New York: Teachers College Press.

Owen, A.E.G. 1971. *Hysteria, Hypnosis, and Healing: The Work of J.M. Charcot*. London: Dennis Dobnson.

Park, L. C. & L. Covi. 1965. Non blind placebo trial: An exploration of neurotic patients' responses to placebo when its inert content is disclosed. *Arch. Gen. Psychiat.* 12: 336-45.

Perls, Fritz. 1969. *Gestalt Therapy Verbatim*. Lafayette, California: Real People Press.

Piaget, Jean. 1952. *The Origins of Intelligence in Children*. NewYork: W. W. Norton & Company.

Pollack, Robert H. & Margaret W. Brenner. 1969. *The Experimental Psychology of Alfred Binet*. New York: Sprnger Publishing Company, Inc.

Ramachandran, V.S. 1993. Behavioral and magnetoencephalographic correlates of plasticity in the adult human brain. *Proc. Natl. Acad. Sci. USA*, Vol. 90. November. 10413-10420.

Rapaport, David, Merton M. Gill & Roy Schafer. 1978. *Diagnostic Psychological Testing*. New York: International University Press, Inc.

Raskin, N.J. 1974. Studies on psychotherapeutic orientation: Ideology in practice. *AAP Psychotherapy Research Monographs*. Orlando, Florida: American Academy of Psychotherapists.

Rogers, Carl R. 1980. *A Way of Being*. Boston: Houghton Mifflin Company.
_____. 1965. *Client Centered Therapy*. Boston: Houghton Mifflin Company.
_____. 1961. *On Becoming a Person*. Boston: Houghton Mifflin Company.
_____. & Barry Stevens. 1967. *Person to Person: The Problem of Being Human. A New Trend in Psychology*. Lafayette, California: Real People Press.

Rosen, Sidney. ed. 1982. *My Voice Will Go with You: The Teaching Tales of Milton H. Erickson*. New York: W. W. Norton & Company.

Rosenthal, R. 1969. Interpersonal expectations: Effects of the experimenter's hypothesis. in *Artifact in Behavioral Research*, ed R. Rosenthal and R. L. Rosnow. New York: Academic Press 181-277.

Rossi, Ernest L., Margaret O. Ryan, & Florence A. Sharp. 1980. *Healing in Hypnosis: The Seminars, Workshops, and Lectures of Milton H. Erickson*. Vol. I. New York: Irvington Publishers, Inc.
_____. _____. & _____. 1985. *Life Reframing in Hypnosis: The Seminars, Workshops, and Lectures of Milton H. Erickson*. Vol. II. New York: Irvington Publishers, Inc.
_____. _____. & _____. 1986. *Mind-Body Communication in Hypnosis: The Seminars, Workshops, and Lectures of Milton H. Erickson*, Vol. III. New York: Irvington Publishers, Inc.
_____. _____. & _____. 1992. *Creative Choice in Hypnosis: The Seminars, Workshops, and Lectures of Milton H. Erickson*. Vol. IV. New York: Irvington Publishers, Inc.

BIBLIOGRAPHY

Schmideberg, Melitta. 1938. The role of suggestion in analytic therapy. *Psychoanalytic Review*. 26: 219-28.

Schofield, W. 1964. *Psychotherapy, the Purchase of Friendship.* Englewood Cliffs, New Jersey: Prentice-Hall, Spectrum Books.

Schoenfeld, J., & A. R. Stone, & S.D. Imber, & S. K. Pande. 1969. Patient-therapist convergence and measures of improvement in short-term psychotherapy. *Psychotherapy: Theory, Research, and Practice*. 6: 267-272.

Shaffer, G. W. & R.S. Lazarus. 1952. *Fundamental Concepts in Clinical Psychology.* New York: McGraw-Hill.

_____. 1956. Hypnosis in supportive therapy. In. *Hypnosis and Its Therapeutic Applications.* by Roy Dorcus. New York: McGraw Hill Book Company, Inc.

Shlien, J.M., Mosak, H.H. and Dreikurs, R. 1962. Effect of time limits: A comparison of two psychotherapies. *Journal of Counseling Psychology*. 31: 24.

Shneidman, Edwin S. 1981. *Endeavors in Psychology: Selections from the Personology of Henry A. Murray.* New York: Harper & Row.

Simpkins, C. A. & Simpkins, A.M. 2000. *Effective Self Hypnosis: Pathways to the Unconscious.* San Diego, California: Radiant Dolphin Press.

_____. & _____. 2000. *Simple Buddhism: A Guide to Enlightened Living.* Boston, Massachusetts: Tuttle Publishing.

_____. & _____. *Simple Taoism: A Guide to Living in Balance.* Boston, Massachusetts: Tuttle Publishing.

_____. & _____. 1999. *Simple Zen: A Guide to Living Moment by Moment.* Boston, Massachusetts: Tuttle Publishing.

_____. & _____. 1996. *Principles of Meditation: Eastern Wisdom for the Western Mind.* Boston, Massachusetts: Tuttle Publishing.

_____, & _____. *An Outcome Comparison Between Indirect Hypnotherapy and Insight Psychotherapy with Consideration Given to Hemisphere Dominance Effect.* Doctoral Dissertation. United States International University, 1983.

Sloane, R. & F. R. Staples, A. H. Cristol, N. J. Yorkston, K. Whipple. 1975. *Psychotherapy versus Behavior Therapy.* Cambridge, Massachusetts: Harvard University Press.

Symonds, Percival M. 1958. *Dynamics of Psychotherapy*. Vol. III. New York: Grune & Stratton.

Thorndike, Edward L. 1931. *Human Learning.* New York: Century Co.

Tillich, Paul. *Dynamics of Faith.* 1957. New York: Harper Torchbooks. Harper & Row.

Torrey, E. Fuller. 1986. *Witchdoctors and Psychiatrists: The Common Roots of Psychotherapy and Its Future.* New York: Harper & Row.

Truax, C. B. and R. R. Carkhuff. 1967. *Toward Effective Counseling and Practice.* Chicago: Aldine.

Vaillant, G.E. 1972. Why men seek psychotherapy. *American Journal of*

Psychiatry. 129: 645-51.

Young, P.C. 1931. Suggestion as indirection. *Journal of Abnormal and Social Psychology.* 26: 69-90.

Whitehorn, John C. 1963. The situation part of diagnosis. *International Journal of Group Psychotherapy.* Vol. XIII. July. 3: 290-299.

_____. 1960. Studies of the doctor as a crucial factor for the prognosis of schizophrenic patients. *International Journal of Psychiatry.* Vol. VI. Nos. 1 & 2 Summer.

_____. 1959. Problems of psychiatric diagnosis. Summer Memorial Lecture, Presented at 44th Scientific Session of the Oregon Medical School Alumni Association. Portland, Oregon. April 10.

_____. & Barbara J. Betz. 1957. A comparison of psychotherapeutic relationships between physicians and schizophrenic patients when insulin is combined with psychotherapy and when psychotherapy is used alone. *American Journal of Psychiatry.* Vol.113. No. 10. April.

_____. 1955. Stress and emotional health. University Lecture, Johns Hopkins University, Baltimore. Feb. 9

_____. 1953. Therapeutic goals and their significance for therapeutic strategy. *Psychiatric Treatment*, Vol. 31. Baltimore: Williams & Wilkins Co.

_____. 1948 Psychotherapy in general medical practice. *Bulletin of the Johns Hopkins Hospital.* Vol. 83, No. 1. January.

_____. The concepts of meaning and cause in psychodynamics. *American Journal of Psychiatry.* 104: 289-297.

_____. 1947. Psychotherapeutic strategy. *Acta. Med. Scand. Suppl.* 196: 626-633.

_____. The doctor's evaluation of patient's attitudes. *Medical Annals of the District of Columbia.* Vol. XII, June. 6: 213-219.

_____. 1944. Guide to interviewing and clinical personality study. *Archives of Neurology and Psychiatry.* 52: 197-216.

_____. 1942. Psychiatry as a basic medical science. *The Connecticut State Medical Journal.* Vol. VI, 9: 693-699.

Winters, Eunice E. ed. 1950. *The Collected Papers of Adolf Meyer: Neurology.* Baltimore: The Johns Hopkins Press.

_____. 1951. *The Collected Papers of Adolf Meyer: Psychiatry.* Baltimore: The Johns Hopkins Press.

_____. 1951. *The Collected Papers of Adolf Meyer: Medical Teaching.* Baltimore: The Johns Hopkins Press.

_____. 1952. *The Collected Papers of Adolf Meyer: Mental Hygiene.* Baltimore: The Johns Hopkins Press.

Zeig, Jeffrey K. ed. 1987. *The Evolution of Psychotherapy.* New York: Brunner/Mazel, Publishers.

_____. 1982. *Ericksonian Approaches to Hypnosis and Psychotherapy.* New York: Brunner/Mazel, Publishers.

_____. ed. 1980. *A Teaching Seminar with Milton H. Erickson.* New York: Brunner/Mazel, Publishers.